HELLENIC STUDIES SERIES 90

EURIPIDES' *INO*

Recent Titles in the Hellenic Studies Series

EURIPIDES' *INO*
COMMENTARY, RECONSTRUCTION, TEXT, AND TRANSLATION

Smaro Nikolaidou-Arampatzi

Center for Hellenic Studies
Trustees for Harvard University
Washington, D.C.
Distributed by Harvard University Press
Cambridge, Massachusetts, and London, England
2022

ISBN: 978-0-674-27255-2
Library of Congress Control Number: 2019021514

Contents

Abbreviations

CPG   E. L. a Leutsch and F. W. Schneidewin. 1839–1851. *Corpus Paroemiograph-orum Graecorum.* 2 vols.

FGrHist   F. Jacoby. 1923–1958. *Die Fragmente der Griechischen Historiker.* Leiden. Repr. 1954–1969.

L-P   E. Lobel and D. L. Page. 1955. *Poetarum Lesbiorum Fragmenta.* Oxford.

LSJ   H. G. Liddell, R. H. Scott, and H. S. Jones. 1996. A *Greek-English Lexicon.* 9th ed. Oxford. Orig. Pub. 1871.

PCG   R. Kassel and C. F. L. Austin. 1983–2001. *Poetae Comici Graeci.* 8 vols. Berlin and New York.

PMG   D. L. Page. 1962. *Poetae Melici Graeci.* Oxford.

TrGF   R. Kannicht, S. L. Radt, and B. Snell. 1971–2004. *Tragicorum Graecorum Fragmenta.* 6 vols. Göttingen.

        Vol. 1. B. Snell. 1971. *Didascaliae Tragicae, Catalogi Tragicorum et Tragoedi-arum, Testimonia et Fragmenra Tragicorum Minorum.* Göttingen.

        Vol. 2. R. Kannicht and B. Snell. 1981. *Fragmenta Adespota.* Göttingen.

        Vol. 3. S. L. Radt. 1985. *Aeschylus.* Göttingen.

        Vol. 4. S. L. Radt. 1999. *Sophocles.* 2nd ed. Göttingen. Orig. pub. 1977.

        Vols. 5.1 and 5.2. R. Kannicht. 2004. *Euripides.* Göttingen.

TrRF   M. Schauer and G. Mannuwald. 2012. *Tragicorum Romanorum Fragmenta.* Göttingen.

        Vol. 1. M. Schauer. 2012. *Livius Andronicus, Naevius, Tragici Minores, Frag-menta Adespota.* Göttingen.

        Vol. 2. G. Mannuwald. 2012. *Ennius.* Göttingen.

Preface

The idea of the reconstruction of Euripides' *Ino* proposed in this study springs from the *Medea* 1282–1289, where the chorus, in trying to fathom Medea's filicide, searches for an equally horrifying precedent and recalls Ino, who, driven mad by Hera, raised her hand murderously to her own children and then committed suicide by leaping into the sea. Since this mythological version—as far as I know—is unknown to us from anywhere else, I think the allusion made by the *Medea's* chorus may be self-referential to Euripides in that Ino's appearance as a filicide refers to one of the poet's earlier works. My idea is supported by Hyginus' *Fabula* 4 entitled *Ino Euripidis*, which begins with an extensive reference to Ino as a maenad on Cithaeron, an element that has remained unexplained in attempts at reconstruction of the play. Certainly, Ino's involvement in maenadic rites exists in Euripides' last play, the *Bacchae*. In this play, Ino, with her other two sisters, Agave and Autonoe, are the leaders of the Theban Bacchic *thiasoi* on Cithaeron, where they celebrate Dionysus and participate in the *sparagmos* of Pentheus, with his mother (Agave) at the head.

The forging of Ino's Dionysiac status begins with her origin. Ino was one of Cadmus' four daughters and the sister of Semele who carried Dionysus after her union with Zeus. After Dionysus' birth from the thigh of Zeus after Semele had been struck by lightning, Hermes entrusted the care of the newborn god to Ino. Ino's role as a nurse of Dionysus infuriated Hera, who inspired mania against their own children in both Ino and her husband Athamas. Athamas, while hunting, mistook for a deer and shot their older son, Learchus. Ino threw their younger son, Melicertes, into a boiling cauldron, and leaped into the sea with the dead child in her arms; then she was metamorphosized into a marine goddess under the name of Leucothea, and Melicertes became the sea god Palaemon.

Belief in Ino as a water deity, who, having won a share of honor from the gods, can benefit humans, appears to have been strong among poets since the epic period. In Homer's *Odyssey* (5.333–353), Leucothea feels pity for Odysseus ('as he wandered and was in sore travail') and arises up from the deep sea to offer him help; she gives him her immortal veil (κρήδεμνον) and advises him on how to reach the land of the Phaeacians, where it is his fate to escape (333–335).[1] Archaic lyric poets honor Ino as a sea goddess, too. In Alcman (fr. 50 PMG), Ino is characterized as ruler of the sea: θαλασσομέδοισ(α). Pindar (*Pythian* 11.2) says that Ino shares the chamber of the Nereids (ὁμοθάλαμος τῶν Νηρηίδων);[2] and elsewhere he emphasizes immortal life given her for all time among the ocean daughters of Nereus in the sea (*Olympian* 2.28–30 λέγοντι δ' ἐν καὶ θαλάσσᾳ / μετὰ κόραισι Νηρῆος ἁλίαις βίοτον ἄφθιτον / Ἰνοῖ τετάχθαι τὸν ὅλον ἀμφὶ χρόνον). In Euripides' *Iphigenia in Tauris*, a brief reference to Ino reminds us of her identity as a sea goddess: when the herdsman meets the unknown Orestes and Pylades arriving at his cave, he prays for help to Palaemon, the son of Leucothea (270–271 ποντίας παῖ Λευκοθέας, νεῶν, δέσποτα Παλαῖμον, ἵλεως ἡμῖν γενοῦ). Even in Lycophron's *Alexandra* 102–107 (in the third century BCE), the honored goddess, to whom Helen sacrifices, is named Bune, probably related to the noun βύνη meaning the sea (Euphorion 127).[3]

On the other hand, Ino's marriage to Athamas is a theme with many mythological versions, in most of which two more wives of Athamas are referred to: Nephele, who bore him Phrixus and Helle, and (/or) Themisto who bore him Erythrius, Leukon, Schoenus, and Ptous. In all narratives, Ino appears to be the second or third wife of Athamas, and, as a stepmother, she is involved in murders against Nephele's and/or Themisto's children. This mythological account of the story of Ino, Athamas, and the Athamantidae can be found only in the work of the later mythographers. Regarding the fifth century BCE, however, in which Euripides' *Ino* was written, we do not know exactly which was the mythological tradition that inspired tragic poets to compose the *mythos* of their plays about Ino, Athamas, and the Athamantidae, from which nothing survives except for some titles and scanty fragments. Only a brief narrative by Herodotus refers to a joint scheme by Ino and Athamas against Phrixus (7.197 ὡς Ἀθάμας ὁ Αἰόλου ἐμηχανήσατο Φρίξῳ μόρον σὺν Ἰνοῖ βουλεύσας). Yet we can guess that the tragedians rather preferred the awful elements of Ino's marital status: her involvement in jealous actions against Athamas' other wives and their children.[4]

As tragic heroine, Ino was rather more important for Euripides, who appears to be the only tragic poet who wrote a tragedy entitled *Ino*. Although the play was surely performed before Aristophanes' *Acharnians* (425 BCE), the

---

[1]   For Ino-Leucothea, Farnell 1916 and 1921:39–47; Finkelberg 2006.
[2]   See Finglass 2007 *ad loc.*
[3]   Etymologicum Magnum 565.45 Εὐφορίων δὲ βύνην τὴν θάλασσαν λέγει. οἷον· "πολύτροφα δάκρυα βύνης" τοὺς ἅλας βουλόμενος εἰπεῖν; Meineken 1823:153.15.
[4]   A considerable attempt to approximate the literary intake of the story of Athamas, Ino, and the Athamantidae has been made recently by Conzález 2017. For a literary and artistic guide on the mythical Ino, see Gantz 1993:176–180; Lyons 2014:122–124.

actual date of its performance remains unknown. Moreover, nothing further is known about the other two Euripides' tragedies that were performed along with the *Ino*. That's why we are fortunate enough to have the mythological narrative of the later Hyginus in his *Fabula* 4, which, under the title *Ino Euripidis*, pledges to concisely convey the events of the play. However, given that there are other narratives by Hyginus referring to the history of Athamas and the Athamantidae, and there is another narrative (*Fabula* 2) of his own called *Ino*, great care is needed, because some elements of the related narratives may have intruded into the narrative of *Fabula* 4. For these reasons, my study will investigate the data of all related narratives and try to find out which of the elements in Hyginus' *Fabula* 4 must be considered reliable for the structure of Euripides' *Ino* and which are to be treated with caution or/and distrust. Above all, I will try to show the importance of Hyginus' reference to Ino's maenadic flight to Cithaeron and her forced return to Athamas' home again.

As one would expect, rebuilding a fragmentary text poses great difficulties. There are even times where there seems to be a need for divine inspiration. However, it is always necessary that our conjectures be based on reason, and the indiscriminate use of imagination avoided. Opposition or even reluctance to the reconstruction work would only be valid if it could be proven that the fragments under reconstruction were not governed by any form of sequence or coherence that would make it possible to link them. However, in my opinion, the reconstruction of a fragmentary play is a purely logical process and a wholly scientific work. In order to achieve this task, our reconstruction proposal should describe a continuation to the surviving fragments of the play. If we consider the original text as a literary depiction of sequential dramatic events, which we assume the poet had in mind, then we can describe the original text by using the surviving fragments as examples of this depiction. It would suffice to find a smooth and coherent interpolation between the extant fragments, a flow that would correspond with our reconstruction proposal. This means that we must establish a compact corpus of dramatic criteria at a thematic and structural level that would describe the continuity in a manner consistent with the flow of the original text. Of course, this corpus must describe a narrative sequence that would apply to the whole text. Thus, between two fragments, the reconstruction proposal would arise from the one that is defined as the *hysteron proteron* fragment, while the second fragment emerges from the proposed interpolation. At the same time, the criterion of fluidity, concerning the way in which the interpolation is to be made, will be ensured by the harmonization of the inserted text with the sequential function it is called upon to fulfill, which means that it is forbidden for us to omit data for the sake of flow.

In this way, any interpolation between the fragments is dictated by the parameters of sequence and fluidity of the proposed text in relation to the original one, which remains unknown. It goes without saying that every reconstruction attempt tries to find links to the surviving plays, and no proposal aspires to be exact in relation to the original play.

Under these terms, the reconstruction of a fragmentary play can be considered well-defined and, consequently, scientifically evaluable. Moreover, most of the works of the tragic poets of antiquity have been lost, and the surviving tragedies of the three major tragic poets (seven plays by Aeschylus, seven by Sophocles, and eighteen by Euripides) are minimal samples of their total work.

Commenting on a fragmentary play is a different task than commenting on a surviving one. In a surviving play, the meaning of the word terms and their function are governed by plot data that are real and unalterable. But in the case of a fragmentary play, the comments on the verbal terms that it rescues need to look for a meaning that will confirm the reconstruction proposal or, at least, will not make it impossible; otherwise, the reconstruction proposal is in doubt. That's why in commenting on a fragmentary text it is not allowed to leave terms undiscussed, especially when their significance is not obvious. Therefore, my commentary on the fragmentary *Ino* will be philological as well as interpretative. In the commentary I use the text of the book fragments edited by Kannicht (TrGF 5.1), and the text of the *Oxyrhynchus Papyrus* 5131 edited by Luppe and Henry.[5] After my reconstruction attempt, the text of both the book fragments and the papyrus is subject to some minor adjustments to previously accepted readings. What changes is the series of the book fragments, which are renumerated. Among them, the papyrus text is placed in the position most likely to be considered. My English translation is in prose. What I have to admit is that my purpose is not to produce an edition of Euripides' *Ino* that would replace the previous reconstruction proposals of the play either with or without comments. My book aims only to offer an edition of Euripides' *Ino* together with a reconsideration of the criteria of the reconstruction of the play, the first after the edition of the *Oxyrhynchus Papyrus* 5131, which has changed radically the reconstruction data of the play. If my proposal holds true, then (a) the dating of the *Ino* can be shifted prior to 431 BCE (the time the *Medea* was performed); (b) the axial point in the play becomes the filicide of Ino who murdered her children in a state of Dionysiac madness; and (c) the filicide of Ino in a state of mania constitutes the dramatic prototype by which the later—perhaps not much—filicide Medea would be judged.

---

[5]   Luppe and Henry 2012.

1

Commentary

1.1 Transmission of the Text

The direct evidence for Euripides' *Ino* comprises twenty-six book fragments (TrGF 5.1 F 398–423) that are excerpts or quotations mostly in the work of Stobaeus (*Ioannis Stobaei Anthologium*). The *Papyrus Strasburg* 304–307, dated to the first half of the third century BCE,[1] has been supposed to contain on the recto lyric parts of Euripides' *Phoenissae, Medea*, and another Euripidean play, which was identified as Euripides' *Ino* by M. Fassino.[2] R. Kannicht (TrGF 5.2 F 953m) includes it among Euripides' fragmenta "incertarum fabularum," but he considers Fassino's identification not to be far from reality ("*Inoni* verisimilius sed non procul dubio recte Fassino 40–43"). The *Oxyrhynchus Papyrus* 5131, dated in the third century CE, was edited in 2012 by W. Luppe and W. B. Henry with the idea that it possibly belongs to Euripides' *Ino*.[3] Two years later, P. Finglass identified this papyrus as a fragment coming from Euripides' *Ino* as such,[4] which perhaps changes radically all the traditional criteria for the reconstruction of the play; moreover, he argued against Fassino's identification of the *Papyrus Strasburg* 304–307 with the *Ino*.[5]

The indirect evidence of the *Ino* is usually limited to Aristophanes' two cursory references in the *Acharnians* 432–434 and the *Wasps* 1412–1414, and one narrative by the Latin mythographer Hyginus (in the second century CE), his *Fabula* 4, entitled *Ino Euripidis*.[6] In my opinion, the indirect evidence of the play should be expanded to include the only extant fragment from Ennius' *Athamas* (TrRF 2 F 42), a fragment of Livius Andronicus' *Ino* (TrRF 1 F 16), and above all

---

[1] Fassino 1999:2–4.
[2] Fassino 1999:40–44.
[3] Luppe and Henry 2012.
[4] Finglass 2014. See Kovacs 2016 for complementary notes.
[5] Finglass 2014:76–77.
[6] One could add evidence existing in the Catalogi Fabularum I (T 6) col. I 21 Εἰνώ, and in some manuscripts of the works quoting fragments of the *Ino*, where the title of the play is referred to as Οἰνεῖ; see TrGF 5.1 32i.

Euripides' *Medea* 1282–1289, the passage in which the chorus refers to Ino as predecessor to Medea's filicide. It is true that Euripides' mythological version of Ino in the *Medea* is unknown from anywhere else; but there are so many traditions that are lost to us.

In his *Acharnians*, produced in 425 BCE, Aristophanes parodies apparently the rags in which Euripides' Ino was costumed, by representing Euripides himself ordering one of his servants, when Dicaeopolis approaches him and begs for a rag:

> ὦ παῖ δὸς αὐτῷ Τηλέφου ῥακώματα.
> κεῖται δ' ἄνωθεν τῶν Θυεστίων ῥακῶν
> μεταξὺ τῶν Ἰνοῦς . . . .
>
> Aristophanes *Acharnians* 432–434

Slave! give him the tatters of Telephus; they are on top of Thyestes' rags, in between them and those of Ino.[7]

In the *Wasps*, produced in 422 BCE, Philocleon makes a mysterious joke by comparing the cadaverous Chaerephon, an associate of Socrates (Plato *Apology* 21a), with the pale Ino suspended from the feet of Euripides:

> . . . . καὶ σὺ δή μοι Χαιρεφῶν
> γυναικὶ †κλητεύειν ἐοικὼς† θαψίνῃ,
> Ἰνοῖ κρεμαμένῃ πρὸς ποδῶν Εὐριπίδου.
>
> Aristophanes *Wasps* 1412–1414

As for you, Chaerephon, can you really be a witness to this woman, when you look like the yellow Ino hanging on Euripides' feet?

Fr. Bothe had proposed that Aristophanes says "Euripides" instead of "Athamas" in order to parody a supplication scene of a Euripidean *Ino* (produced earlier), in which the regretful Ino implores Athamas' mercy.[8] Certainly, this Aristophanic passage makes a supplication scene in Euripides' *Ino* not impossible. However, the comic comparison itself gives us no real information about the play it comes from. A. Sommerstein, who accepts Bothe's emendation, considers that Aristophanes brilliantly interchanges Athamas with Euripides, because the luck of an actor/actress (his/her theatrical success or failure) hangs on the poet

---

[7]   Translations are my own unless otherwise indicated.

[8]   Bothe 1844:145. Bothe's emendation has been widely accepted; see Webster 1967:98; also the commentaries (*ad Wasps* 1414) by McDowell 1971 and Sommerstein 1983.

himself and not on another actor/actress.[9] Sommerstein's observation sheds light on the surprise appearance of Euripides' name at the end of the verse. The way to this observation was paved by A. Matthiae, who had argued that Aristophanes' parody lies in the metaphorical meaning of the participle κρεμαμένη in this passage.[10] As it seems, the surprise appearance of Euripides' name at the end of the passage is an element that "may itself be the whole of the joke."[11] What we need not to forget is the theatrical evidence itself: in this comic scene Chaerephon appears on stage as a witness on behalf of a baker's wife who is mocked by the unjust Philocleon. With this as a given, it is more probable that the dative γυναικί (referring to the baker's wife) joins with the verb κλητεύεις (as its object), and that the epithet θαψίνη qualifies only the following word Ἰνοῖ. Perhaps the comic comparison of Chaerephon with the yellow Ino, together with the participle κρεμαμένη, convey an extreme misfortune of the Euripidean Ino, for which the poet is criticized by Aristophanes.[12] A similar impression is implied by the parody in the *Acharnians*, where Ino's rags seem to express her ultimate misfortune.

Hyginus' evidence for Euripides' *Ino* exists in the following narrative:[13]

Athamas in Thessalia rex, cum Inonem uxorem, ex qua duos filios <susceperat>, perisse putaret, duxit †nymphae filiam Themistonem uxorem; ex ea geminos filios procreavit. postea resciit Inonem in Parnaso esse, quam bacchationis causa eo pervenisse; misit qui eam adducerent; quam adductam celavit. resciit Themisto eam inventam esse, sed quae esset nesciebat. coepit velle filios ejus necare; rei consciam quam captivam esse credebat ipsam Inonem sumpsit, et ei dixit ut filios suos candidis vestimentis operiret, Inonis filios nigris. Ino suos candidis, Themistonis pullis operuit; tunc Themisto decepta suos filios occidit; id ubi resciit, ipsa se necavit. Athamas autem in venatione per insaniam Learchum majorem filium suum interfecit, at Ino cum minore filio Melicerte in mare se dejecit et dea est facta.

Hyginus *Fabula* 4

King Athamas of Thessaly thought that his wife, Ino, by whom he had fathered two sons, was dead. So, he married Themisto, the daughter of a Nymph, and had twin sons by her. Later, he learned that Ino was

---

[9] Sommerstein 1983:242.
[10] Matthiae 1829:196.
[11] See Farmer 2017:146–147.
[12] Scholia Aristophanes *Wasps* 1413b (II 1.223 Koster) εἰσήγαγε γὰρ Εὐριπίδης τὴν Ἰνὼ ὠχρὰν ὑπὸ τῆς κακοπαθείας (the text from TrGF 5.1 32 testimonium iib p. 442).
[13] Text from Marshall 2002.

on Mount Parnassus; she had gone there to celebrate the Bacchic mysteries. He sent men to bring her back, and when they had, he kept her out of view. Themisto learned that they had found a woman but did not know who she was. Themisto planned to kill Ino's sons and took as her accomplice Ino herself (who, she thought, was just a captive girl), and told her to dress her sons in white and Ino's in black. Ino dressed her own in white clothing and Themisto's in black. Misled in this fashion, Themisto killed her own sons. When she realized her error, she committed suicide. As for Athamas, in a fit of madness he killed his elder son, Learchus, while hunting. Ino threw herself into the sea along with her younger son, Melicertes, and was made a goddess.[14]

This special narrative, promising to record the plot of Euripides' *Ino*, refers to a mythical account, namely Ino's maenadic flight to Cithaeron, which is unknown from anywhere else. From the way the events are arranged in it, we suppose that Ino's flight from her house and Athamas' subsequent marriage to Themisto belonged to the background of the play. The plot would rather begin with Ino's arrest on Cithaeron, ordered by Athamas; and it would comprise Ino's forced return to her home, her secret servitude to Themisto, and her deceitful participation in Themisto's conspiring, which would culminate in Themisto's unconscious filicide and her subsequent suicide. The last events of the narrative, referring to Athamas' killing of their older son, Learchus, in hunting, and Ino's jumping into the sea with their younger son, Melicertes, are relevant to the well-known mythical account of Hera's *ira* against Ino. They are also found as such at the ending point of Hyginus' *Fabula* 2, entitled *Ino*, which narrates the general account of the mythical Ino; but, they are absent from Hyginus' *Fabula* 1, entitled *Themisto*, which narrates Themisto's unconscious filicide against her own children. Therefore, it is not safe to suppose that in *Fabula* 4 the events of Hera's *ira* against Ino are narrated as the ending events of her name play by Euripides. As usually happens in mythographic works of late antiquity, Hyginus' *Fabula* 4 not improbably incorporated some more mythological elements. What we need to discuss is if the mythical account of Hera's *ira* is sufficiently relevant to the key theme of the narrative of *Fabula* 4; otherwise, it is unsafe to rely on.[15]

The single extant fragment from Ennius' *Athamas* describes an orgiastic celebration of a female Bacchic *thiasos*, who unexpectedly (?) either join with

---

[14] Translation by Smith and Trzaskoma 2007.
[15] For credibility gaps in Hyginus' narratives, see Huys 1996 and 1997. For the ending of the *Fabula* 4 in particular, Bursian 1866:776; Schmidt 1872; Nauck 1889; Luppe 1984; Wilamowitz-Moellendorff 1931–1932:218n3; disagreement (with Bursian and Schmidt) by Rose 1933.

or are interrupted by a second group of young—probably transfigured—men crying and dancing for Dionysus in the same manner:

> <h>is erat in ore Bromius, his Bacchus pater,
> illis Lyaeus vitis inventor sacrae
> tum pariter † euhan euhium †
> ignotus iuvenum coetus alterna vice
> inibat alacris Bacchico insulta<n>s modo.

Ennius Athamas TrRF 2 F 42

In their lips was Bromius, in theirs Bacchus Father, in others Lyaeus, the discoverer of the sacred vine, when, also crying *euhan euhoe,* an unknown transfigured troop of youths began to enter eagerly, jumping in Bacchic manner.

This fragment is quoted by Charisius *Grammar* I p. 241. 3–11 Keil = p. 314 Bar, on *euhoe.* Verses 1–2 refer to a maenadic chorus invoking Dionysus as Bromius, Bacchus, and Lyaeus. From the later many names of Dionysus (Ovid *Metamorphoses* 4.11–17), Attic tragedy had Βρόμιος (e.g. Aeschylus *Eumenides* 24 Βρόμιος ἔχει τὸν χῶρον), Βάκχος (e.g. Sophocles *Oedipus Tyrannus* 211 οἰνῶπα Βάκχον, εὔιον), and Εὔιος (Euripides *Bacchae* 157 εὔια τὸν εὔιον ἀγαλλόμεναι θεὸν). The name Λυαῖος (/ Λυσαῖος) is not found before Leonidas of Tarentum (*Anthologia Palatina* 6.154.1).[16] However, in Euripides' *Bacchae* we can read a detailed presentation of Dionysus as Λυαῖος (/ Λυσαῖος), the god who releases wretched mortals from their troubles with the forgetful power of wine:

> ὃς δ' ἦλθ' ἔπειτ', ἀντίπαλον ὁ Σεμέλης γόνος
> βότρυος ὑγρὸν πῶμ' ηὗρε κἀσηνέγκατο
> 280 θνητοῖς, ὃ παύει τοὺς ταλαιπώρους βροτοὺς
> λύπης, ὅταν πλησθῶσιν ἀμπέλου ῥοῆς,
> ὕπνον τε λήθην τῶν καθ' ἡμέραν κακῶν
> δίδωσιν, οὐδ' ἔστ' ἄλλο φάρμακον πόνων.

Euripides Bacchae 278–283

Next came he, the son of Semele, who discovered a good equivalent (to the good of Demeter), the liquid drink of the grape, and introduced it to mortals, that which releases wretched people from sorrow; when they

---

[16] Jocelyn 1967 comments (*ad* 120–121) that republican Latin drama has the names *Bromius* and *Bacchus* but not *Lyaeus.*

get drunk with the stream of the vine, they are given sleep and forget the evils of the day. There is no other medicine for suffering, none.[17]

Therefore, in the Ennius' *Athamas* fragment, line 2 may be considered a precise synopsis of the Euripidean passage from the *Bacchae* describing the Lyaeus Dionysus. Moreover, the Bacchic cries *euhan euhium* in line 3 match with *Bacchae* 157 (εὖια τὸν εὖιον ἀγαλλόμεναι θεόν);[18] and the male Bacchic group in lines 4–5, who are alleged to participate in the *orgia*, may recall Cadmus' and Teiresias' Bacchic appearance in the first episode of the *Bacchae* (especially verses 178–209). The ablative *alterna vice*, in particular, may show either that the members of the male group utter their Bacchic cries in alternation (while they enter in the celebration place) or that they are transfigured into maenads; the latter underlines their female transformation, a fact that is especially exalted in the Pentheus' transfiguration scene in the *Bacchae* (913–976). Based on what Hyginus narrates in his *Fabula* 4, O. Ribbeck connects the fragment from Ennius' *Athamas* with Euripides' *Ino*.[19] In particular, he supposes that the preserved verses belong to a messenger speech reporting Ino's maenadism and her arrest on Cithaeron. We understand that Ino's maenadism in her name play of Euripides is a possible element, which became attractive for Ennius, though his tragedy is not entitled *Ino*, but *Athamas*.

From Livius Andronicus' *Ino* only a few verses survive, quoted by Terentius Maurus 1931–1938 (Keil) in an example of the meter μείουρος:[20]

> Livius ille vetus Graio cognomine suae
> inserit Inoni versus, puto, tale docimen:
> praemisso heroo subiungit namque miuron,
> hymnum quando chorus festo canit ore Triviae.
> 5 et jam purpureo suras include cothurno,
> balteus et revocet volucres in pectore sinus,
> pressaque jam gravida crepitent tibi terga pharetra
> derige odorisequos ad certa cubilia canes.
>
> Livius Andronicus *Ino* TrRF 1 F 16

That ancient poet Livius, known by his Greek surname, inserts, I think, some verses in his *Ino*, tested by the following document. Precisely, after an initial heroic proemium, he adds a *meiuron*, at the moment the

---

[17] Translation by Seaford 1996.
[18] For the restoration of the text see Jocelyn 1967 and Manuwald 2015:17–18.
[19] Ribbeck 1875:204–205.
[20] μείουρος is called the meter, the last foot of which is a pyrrhic or iambus.

chorus chants a hymn in the festivity of the Trivia shore. "Now is the time to put your shin in the purple boot (*kothornos*), the waist belt of your garment to stir up the innermost cravings on your chest, your loaded backs to make sounds from the stuffy quiver, to lead the dogs that sniff to the sure places."

The quoted verses (5–8) are alleged to be part of a hymn to Artemis, in which the chorus of Livius Andronicus' *Ino* animatedly exhorts a person to proceed to the chase. We might suppose that these verse lines introduced Athamas' killing of his older son in hunting, according to the mythical account of Hera's ira against Ino and Athamas, which, in all probability, was part of the dramatic plot of the play. Ribbeck identifies the plot of Livius Andronicus' *Ino* with that of Ennius' *Athamas*, in which he includes, as I mentioned, a scene referring to Ino's maenadism on Cithaeron. However, he does not explain how Ino's maenadism could be connected with the events of Hera's ira against her and Athamas in the plot of the same play, either Ennius' *Athamas* or Livius Andronicus' *Ino*.

The detecting of all these Bacchic elements in a possible Euripidean tradition of Ino show us the way to the *Medea* 1282–1289, where the chorus recalls the frenzied Ino as the only filicide woman precedent to Medea:[21]

> μίαν δὴ κλύω μίαν τῶν πάρος
> γυναῖκ' ἐν φίλοις χέρα βαλεῖν τέκνοις,
> Ἰνὼ μανεῖσαν ἐκ θεῶν, ὅθ' ἡ Διὸς
> 1285 δάμαρ νιν ἐξέπεμψε δωμάτων ἄλαις·
> πίτνει δ' ἁ τάλαιν' ἐς ἅλμαν φόνῳ
> τέκνων δυσσεβεῖ,
> ἀκτῆς ὑπερτείνασα ποντίας πόδα,
> δυοῖν τε παίδοιν ξυνθανοῦσ' ἀπόλλυται.

Euripides Medea 1282–1289

One woman, only one, of all that have been, I do hear of who put her hand to her beloved children: Ino who was inspired with mania by the gods, when the wife of Zeus drove her from her house to wander raging. The unfortunate woman fell into the sea because of the wicked murder of her children. Jumping high above the sea's edge, she perished, following her two children to death.

---

[21] See Page 1938 *ad* 1284; Eisner 1979:158–159.

Since this mythological version is unknown from anywhere else and scholars remain unable to find its source,[22] I consider it to be the strongest evidence of Euripides' *Ino*, with the idea that the chorus of the *Medea* here may directly recall a tragic version, that of the filicide Ino, staged by Euripides himself earlier. The fact that Euripides' *Ino* is parodied by Aristophanes at the *Acharnians* 432–434 (first performed in 425 BCE) does not necessarily mean that the play was produced shortly before 425 BCE (e.g. in 426 BCE); nor do metrical resolutions help to specify the date of its original performance.[23] The crucial element is Ino's filicide that is referred to results from divine madness and expulsion from home, which might be paralleled to her maenadic flight to Cithaeron recorded in Hyginus' *Fabula* 4,[24] despite that in the *Medea* it is Hera who inspires Ino's mania and not Dionysus. In the *Heracles*, too, the title hero unwillingly kills his own wife and children under the mania inspired in him by Hera (through Lyssa), but his situation is characterized with Bacchic wording (878–879 μανιάσιν λύσσαις / χορευθέντ' ἐναύλοις, 889 κατάρχεται χορεύματ', 966 φόνος σ' ἐβάκχευσεν νεκρῶν, 1142 βάκχευσ') culminating in his characterization as a *Bacchos* of Hades (1119 Ἅιδου βάκχος εἶ).[25]

1.2 Text and Commentary

1.2.1 Book Fragments (TrGF 5.1. 32. F 398–423 Kannicht)

Fragment 398

> εὕδουσα δ' Ἰνοῦς συμφορὰ πολὺν χρόνον
> νῦν ὄμμ' ἐγείρει

In the Scolia ad Pindar *Isthmian* 4.39a Drachmann (ἐκ λεχέων ἀνάγει φάμαν παλαιὰν εὐκλέων ἔργων· ἐν ἔργῳ γὰρ πέσεν), fr. 398 is attributed to Euripides as an expression parallel to the Pindaric ἀλλ' ἀνεγειρομένα ... λάμπει. The fragment

---

[22] Schwartz 1891 *ad Medea* 1284: οἱ μὲν ἱστοροῦσι τῷ παιδὶ συγκατενεχθῆναι τὴν Ἰνὼ εἰς τὴν θάλασσαν· Εὐριπίδης δέ φησιν αὐτὴν αὐτόχειρα τῶν δύο παίδων γενομένην, Λεάρχου καὶ Μελικέρτου, αὐτὴν ὕστερον εἰς τὴν θάλασσαν ῥῖψαι. Newton 1985 suggests that Ino's maniac filicide in the *Medea* is a version invented by Euripides himself; the spectators accept it as a poetic licence with the sentiment that the chorus would not cite an event that never occurred. See also Mastronarde 2002 *ad Medea* 1284.

[23] Cropp and Fick 1985:81; see Finglass 2014:70n35.

[24] Cf. the Theban women's flight from their homes to Cithaeron after they had been inspired mania by Dionysus himself in the *Bacchae* 32–33 τοιγάρ νιν αὐτὰς ἐκ δόμων ᾤστρησ' ἐγώ / μανίαις, ὄρος δ' οἰκοῦσι παράκοποι φρενῶν. Zeitlin 2008:320 considers the Euripidean *Ino* "an explicitly Dionysiac play" because of Ino's flight to Cithaeron referred to by Hyginus.

[25] For relevance of Ino to Heracles' situation, see Lyons 2014:64–67.

was first connected with the Euripidean *Ino* by Valckenaer 173. In all probability, it belongs to the prologue of the play (*duce* Musgrave 567 and *probante* Welcker 618). Finglass prefers to class it among the "fragmenta incertis dramatis."[26]

1. εὔδουσα (asleep, sleeping) is the emendation by Musgrave (cf. Welcker 618), based on Plutarch *Antonius* 36.1: εὔδουσα δ᾽ ἡ δεινὴ συμφορὰ χρόνον πολύν, ὁ Κλεοπάτρας ἔρως, δοκῶν κατηυνάσθαι καὶ κατακεκλῆσθαι τοῖς βελτίοσι λογισμοῖς, αὖθις ἀνέλαμπε καὶ ἀνεθάρρει.[27] The verb εὔδειν here is used metaphorically, with the meaning of being calm (inoperative / not dangerous / harmless / inoffensive). Cf. Homer *Iliad* 5.524 (ἀτρέμας, ὄφρ᾽ εὕδησι μένος Βορέαο καὶ ἄλλων), for the might of the North Wind; Simonides 371.22 Page 1968 (εὑδέτω δὲ πόντος, εὑδέτω δ᾽ ἄμετρον κακόν), for the sea and the evil; Solon 4.19 West 1980 (ἢ στάσιν ἔμφυλον πόλεμόν θ᾽ εὕδοντα ἐπεγείρει), for civil war; Plato *Phaedrus* 267a (Τισίαν δὲ Γοργίαν τε ἐάσομεν εὕδειν), for undisturbed persons; Theocritus *Idylls* 2.126 (εὖδόν τ᾽ εἴ κε μόνον τὸ καλὸν στόμα τεῦς ἐφίλησα), for calming down.

2. ὄμμ᾽(α) ἐγείρει (wakes and stirs up / is roused) is metaphorical, implying that Ino now is expected to become offensive and dangerous. Pindar *Isthmian* 3.41 (ἐν ὕπνῳ γὰρ πέσεν· ἀλλ᾽ ἀνεγειρομένα χρῶτα λάμπει) and Cicero *For Sestius* 68 (*res erat et causa nostra eo jam loci, ut erigere oculos et vivere videretur*) are considered to be parallel expressions.[28]

Fragment 399

> φίλαι γυναῖκες, πῶς ἂν ἐξ ἀρχῆς δόμους
> Ἀθάμαντος οἰκήσαιμι τῶν πεπραγμένων
> δράσασα μηδέν;

Plutarch's interpretation (*De Sera Numinis Vindicta* 11 [556 a]), provided in his passage (which saves the fragment), refers to Ino's remorse for her past deeds (ὥσπερ τῆς Ἰνοῦς ἀκούομεν ἐν τοῖς θεάτροις λεγούσης, ἐφ᾽ οἷς ἔδρασε μεταμελομένης). The reason for her repentance, in Plutarch's view, is for her prior offenses of which Ino was fully aware and which she should have regretted (ταῦτα εἰκὸς ἑκάστου τῶν πονηρῶν τὴν ψυχὴν ... διαλογίζεσθαι, πῶς ἂν ἐκβᾶσα τῆς μνήμης τῶν ἀδικημάτων καὶ τὸ συνειδὸς ἐξ ἑαυτῆς ἐκβαλοῦσα ... βίον ἄλλον ἐξ ἀρχῆς βιώσειεν). The fragment was connected with the Euripidean Ino by Valckenaer 173, whose idea is generally accepted.[29]

---

[26] Finglass 2016:300n3.
[27] Webster 1967:99.
[28] Welcker 1839–1841:2.618n5.
[29] di Gregorio 1980:59–60.

1. φίλαι γυναῖκες: a vocative addressing, in all probability, the female chorus of the play. Cf. *Helen* 255 (φίλαι γυναῖκες, τίνι πότμῳ συνεζύγην;); *Medea* 214 (Κορίνθιαι γυναῖκες, εξῆλθον δόμων); *Hippolytus* 373 (Τροιζήνιαι γυναῖκες, αἳ τόδ᾽ ἔσχατον).

ἐξαρχῆς means πάλιν. Cf. Aristophanes *Plutus* 221 οὐκ ἤν γε πλουτήσωσιν ἐξ ἀρχῆς πάλιν.

1-2. πῶς ἂν ... οἰκήσαιμι (;): the optative mood, followed by the potential ἄν, refers to the present and future of Ino in Athamas' house. It points to the real situation she faces, and which she feels unable to endure. If it was simply embarrassment or bewilderment that characterized Ino's situation, the subjunctive mood (πῶς οἰκήσω;) would have been sufficient.

2. τῶν πεπραγμένων: Among Ino's previous actions what has a prominent place is her plotting against Phrixus and Helle, the children of Athamas with his first wife, Nephele.[30] But here we may think of Ino's maenadic deeds in Cithaeron, from where Athamas has just brought her back.

Fragment 400

> ὦ θνητὰ πράγματ᾽, ὦ γυναικεῖαι φρένες·
> ὅσον νόσημα τὴν Κύπριν κεκτήμεθα.

This fragment is cited by Stobaeus 4.22.183 (4.559.1 Hense) as ψόγος γυναικῶν. It refers to female love as a disease, by implying strong emotion through the quantative adverb ὅσον (applied to νόσημα) and the perfect tense κεκτήμεθα. The idea of love as a disease is rather a *locus communis*. Detailed descriptions are there in the archaic lyric poets referring to emotions of both men and women (Archilochus fr. 193 West 1980 δύστηνος ἔγκειμαι πόθῳ, / ἄψυχος, χαλεπῇσι θεῶν ὀδύνῃσιν ἔκητι / πεπαρμένος δι᾽ ὀστέων). Especially, in a well-known fragment of Sappho, the description of the symptoms of love on the lover's body are described as an outburst of emotions.[31] In tragedy, characterizations of love as a disease are referred only to women; and they are found mostly in the plays of Euripides; especially in *Hippolytus* (40, 121–309, 394, 474–479, 512, 597, 698, 766) the disease symptoms of Phaedra's love of Hippolytus are paradigmatic.[32]

---

[30] Welcker 1839–1841:2.619.
[31] Sappho fr. 199.5–16 Page 1968 (= 31.5–15 L–P); only indicatively, I cite verses 9–12 ἀλλ᾽ ἄκαν μὲν γλῶσσα †ἔαγε†, λέπτον / δ᾽ αὔτικα χρῶι πῦρ ὑπαδεδρόμηκεν, / ὀππάτεσσι δ᾽ οὐδ᾽ ἔν ὄρημμ᾽, ἐπιρρόμ- / βεισι δ᾽ ἄκουαι.
[32] See Barrett 1964:182, 195, 200; Zeitlin 1985:59–63, 106–110.

Fragment 401

> φεῦ,
> ὅσῳ τὸ θῆλυ δυστυχέστερον γένος
> πέφυκεν ἀνδρῶν· ἔν τε τοῖσι γὰρ καλοῖς
> πολλῷ λέλειπται κἀπὶ τοῖς αἰσχροῖς πλέον

Fr. 401 is cited by Stobaeus 4.22.182 (4.558.18 Hense). It speaks about female inferiority with a spirit of strong antithesis to men. In Euripides' *Ino*, this antithesis might be especially understood in the framework of the maenadic antithesis to male, given that Hyginus' *Fabula* 4 pays great attention to the fact that Ino was a maenad, who—rather unwillingly—was transferred back by Athamas to her home. Enmity of the maenads towards male is often depicted in Attic vases, where they attack the satyrs with their *thyrsoi*.[33] Cf. the passage from Euripides' *Bacchae* 762–764 (κεῖναι δὲ θύρσους ἐξανιεῖσαι χερῶν / ἐτραυμάτιζον κἀπενώτιζον φυγῇ / γυναῖκες ἄνδρας οὐκ ἄνευ θεῶν τινος) in the first messenger's narrative (731–764), describing the Theban maenads' attack against their male hunters on Cithaeron with Agave as their leader (732 θηρώμεθ' ἀνδρῶν τῶνδ' ὕπ'· ἀλλ' ἕπεσθέ μοι).

Fragment 402

> νόμοι γυναικῶν οὐ καλῶς κεῖνται πέρι·
> χρῆν γὰρ τὸν εὐτυχοῦνθ' ὅτι πλείστας ἔχειν
> {γυναῖκας, εἴπερ τροφὴ δόμοις παρῆν},
> 4   ὡς τὴν κακὴν μὲν ἐξέβαλλε δωμάτων,
> τὴν δ' οὖσαν ἐσθλὴν ἡδέως ἐσῴζετο.
> νῦν δ' εἰς μίαν βλέπουσι, κίνδυνον μέγαν
> ῥίπτοντες· οὐ γὰρ τῶν τρόπων πειρώμενοι
> 8   νύμφας ἐς οἴκους ἑρματίζονται βροτοί

Fr. 402 is cited by Stobaeus 4.22.36 (4.516.1 Hense) as a passage explaining why marriage is an evil (ὅτι οὐκ ἀγαθὸν τὸ γαμεῖν). The idea of male priority over female here is interwoven with sophisticated ideas about priority of polygamy over monogamy. The speaker would be Athamas or one of his wives (Themisto or Ino);[34] the latter would express these ideas in a spirit of strong irony, in my opinion.

---

[33] McNally 1984:132–138 (especially).
[34] Welcker 1839–1841:2.622–623 prefers Ino (addressing Themisto) to Athamas as a speaker of these lines.

2. χρῆν is Scaliger's emendation of the scriptum χρή in Stobaeus. The present tense χρή expresses reality. The imperfect tense χρῆν is in accordance with ἐξέβαλλε (4) and ἐσῴζετο (5), and expresses an impossible situation which, however, could be probable.

ἔχειν is emended to γαμεῖν by Nauck 1889 and to τρέφειν by Headlam 1893:93.

3. The text in verse line 3 is interpolated in the third iambic meter, where the first long syllable is absent. The verse line is deleted by Mekler. Emendations proposed are εἴπερ <ἂν> τροφὴ (Schwyzer 2.350); εἴπερ <δὴ> τροφὴ (Stobaeus ms. Paris 1985); εἴπερ <ἡ> τροφὴ (Gesner); εἴπερ <ἐν> δόμοις τροφῇ (Pflugk); εἴπερ δώμασιν τροφῇ (Nauck'). See TrGF 5.1 *ad loc.*

4-5. Cf. *Hippolytus* 930-931 ὡς ἡ φρονοῦσα τἄδικ' ἐξηλέγχετο / πρὸς τῆς δικαίας, κοὐκ ἂν ἠπατώμεθα.

6-7. Cf. *Heracleidae* 148-149 δεῦρ' ἦλθον ἢ κίνδυνον ἐξ ἀμηχάνων / ῥίπτοντες... (and Elmsley 1813 *ad loc.*); *Rhesus* 154-155 ἐγὼ πρὸ γαίας τόνδε κίνδυνον θέλω / ῥίψας κατόπτης ναῦς ἐπ' Ἀργείων μολεῖν.

8. ἑρματίζονται: "velut sabburam recipient" (Musgrave 567). Cf. fr. 689.1-2 οὐδεὶς δ' ἐς οἴκους δεσπότας ἀμείνονας / αὐτοῦ πρίασθαι βούλεται (from the *Syleus Satyricus*); Lycophron *Alexandra* 1319 εἰς τὴν λάληθρον κίσσαν ἡρματίξατο (and Wilamowitz 1924:2.160).

Athamas' claim echoes the sophist Antiphon (fr. B49 Diels) who lamented that marriage is a big contest for mankind (μέγας γὰρ ἀγὼν ὁ γάμος ἀνθρώπῳ). In tragedies, which are rather contemporary with the *Ino*, there is awareness about monogamous marriage. In Sophocles' *Antigone* (performed at 442 BCE), Ismene claims to Creon that no other woman would be fitted to Haimon as her sister was (570 οὐχ ὥς γ' ἐκείνῳ τῇδέ τ' ἦν ἡρμοσμένα); in Sophocles' *Trachiniae* (which remains undated but was probably produced between 440 and 430 BCE), Deianeira attempts to deter Heracles from loving his young captive, Iole, but unwillingly causes his death; and in Euripides' *Medea* (performed in 431 BCE), the title heroine consciously kills her own children at the culminating point of her jealous agency against her unfaithful husband, Jason. There is a paradigm of polygamy, when, after the Sicilian Expedition, Athens temporarily changed the law and permitted a man two wives for the city to be repopulated.[35] In the

---

[35] Diogenes Laertius 2.26 (= Aristotle *On Good Birth* fr. 93 Ross) Φησὶ δ' Ἀριστοτέλης δύο γυναῖκας αὐτὸν (Σωκράτην) ἀγαγέσθαι· προτέραν μὲν Ξανθίππην, ἐξ ἧς αὐτῷ γενέσθαι Λαμπροκλέα· δευτέραν δὲ Μυρτώ, τὴν Ἀριστείδου τοῦ δικαίου θυγατέρα, ἣν καὶ ἄπροικον λαβεῖν, ἐξ ἧς γενέσθαι Σωφρονίσκον καὶ Μενέξενον. οἱ δὲ προτέραν γῆμαι τὴν Μυρτώ φασιν· ἔνιοι δὲ καὶ ἀμφοτέρας σχεῖν ὁμοῦ, ὧν ἐστι Σάτυρός τε καὶ Ἱερώνυμος ὁ Ῥόδιος. φασὶ γὰρ βουληθέντας Ἀθηναίους διὰ τὸ λειπανδρεῖν συναυξῆσαι τὸ πλῆθος, ψηφίσασθαι γαμεῖν μὲν ἀστὴν μίαν, παιδοποιεῖσθαι δὲ καὶ ἐξ ἑτέρας· ὅθεν τοῦτο ποιῆσαι καὶ Σωκράτην. Cf. Plutarch *Aristides* 27.2; *Suda s.v. leipandrein.* On the date of the decree and its content, Harrison 1968-1971:1.16-17;

fourth century, Lysias (3.6) praises the well-ordered life of his sister and nieces in their household (ἔνδον οὐσῶν τῆς τε ἀδελφῆς τῆς ἐμῆς καὶ τῶν ἀδελφιδῶν, αἳ οὕτω κοσμίως βεβιώκασιν ὥστε καὶ ὑπὸ τῶν οἰκείων ὁρώμεναι αἰσχύνεσθαι); and the orator Lycurgus (fr. 3 Conomis) warns that, when a woman is deprived of her marital harmony, the rest of her life becomes lifeless (ὅταν γυνὴ ὁμονοίας τῆς πρὸς ἄνδρα στερηθῇ, ἀβίωτος ὁ καταλειπόμενος γίγνεται βίος). On the other hand, Plato recommends public education and public office for women for the welfare of the State, though he considers the female to be generically inferior to the male (*Laws* 781c ὅσῳ δὲ ἡ θήλεια ἡμῖν φύσις ἐστὶ πρὸς ἀρετὴν χείρων τῆς τῶν ἀρρένων, τοσούτῳ διαφέρει πρὸς τὸ πλέον ἢ διπλάσιον εἶναι. τοῦτ' οὖν ἐπαναλαβεῖν καὶ ἐπανορθώσασθαι καὶ πάντα συντάξασθαι κοινῇ γυναιξί τε καὶ ἀνδράσιν ἐπιτηδεύματα βέλτιον πρὸς πόλεως εὐδαιμονίαν).

Fragment 403

τίς ἄρα μήτηρ ἢ πατὴρ κακὸν μέγα
βροτοῖς ἔφυσε τὸν δυσώνυμον φθόνον;
ποῦ καί ποτ' οἰκεῖ σώματος λαχὼν μέρος;
4   ἐν χερσὶν ἢ σπλάγχνοισιν ἢ παρ' ὄμματα;
† ἔσθ' ἡμῖν ὡς ἦν μόχθος ἰατροῖς μέγας
τομαῖς ἀφαιρεῖν ἢ ποτοῖς ἢ φαρμάκοις
πασῶν μεγίστην τῶν ἐν ἀνθρώποις νόσων

Fr. 403 is cited by Stobaeus 3.38.8 (3.709.9 Hense) π. φθόνου as a paradigmatic description of *phthonos* (envy).

1–2. Cf. Hesiod *Theogony* 211–232.

2. δυσώνυμον: ill-sounding. Verse line 2 is used by Aelian *De natura animalium* 3.17 (1.66.14 Hercher λέγει ... Εὐριπίδης δυσώνυμον {ὄντα Hercher} τὸν φθόνον) in order to explain why (or how) *phthonos* is characterized δυσώνυμος.[36]

3–4. According to Satyrus Historicus *Vita Euripidis* (*Oxyrhynchus Papyrus* 9.1176 fr. 39 col. 30), verses 3–4 were parodied by the comic poet Atticus imitating Epicharmus.

Euripides' description of human envy as an illness echoes current medical procedures (surgery, medical remedies) and anatomical interest in locating the illness home in the parts of human body. The medical remedies referred to are probably scientific, though the division between ποτοῖς and φαρμάκοις in verse

---

Ogden 1996:72–75. On the interpretation of the decree and its legitimate reproductive arrangements, see Lape 2010:263–273.
[36] For onstage *phthonos* in Greek drama, see the socio-psychological approach by Sanders 2014:118–129, 130–168 (for sexual jealousy in classical Athens).

line 6 implies that folk remedies are not excluded.[37] Cf. fr. 1072 (μέλλων τ' ἰατρὸς τῇ νόσῳ διδοὺς χρόνον / ἰάσατ' ἤδη μᾶλλον ἢ τεμὼν χρόα) defending the anti-surgery new trend of the time (in the spirit of the Hippocratic idea of *kairos*; and Gorgias' *Helen* 14, for scientific remedies).[38] The verse lines of fr. 403 are probably to be spoken by Athamas, crying about female jealousy (Ino's and/or Themisto's jealousy).

Fragment 404

τό τ' εὐγενές
πολλὴν δίδωσιν ἐλπίδ' ὡς ἄρξουσι γῆς

Fragment 405

τὴν εὐγένειαν, κἂν ἄμορφος ᾖ γάμος,
τιμῶσι πολλοὶ προσλαβεῖν τέκνων χάριν
τό τ' ἀξίωμα μᾶλλον ἢ τὰ χρήματα

Frr. 404 and 405 are cited by Stobaeus (4.29.48 [5.721.13 Hense] and 4.29.49 [5.721.16 Hense] respectively) as speaking about nobility (π. εὐγενείας). Their gnomological content (about nobility and noble birth) fits well in Athamas' arguments; but they could also be spoken by Ino or Themisto, explaining the criteria of their marriage to the king Athamas.

Fragment 406

μὴ σκυθρωπὸς ἴσθ' ἄγαν
πρὸς τοὺς κακῶς πράσσοντας, ἄνθρωπος γεγώς

Fr. 406 is cited by Stobaeus 4.48.4 (5.1009.6 Hense) as saying that we should not gloat over misfortunes of other people (ὅτι οὐ χρὴ ἐπιχαίρειν τοῖς ἀτυχοῦσι). Σκυθρωπός usually characterizes a sulky face (e.g. *Medea* 271 σὲ τὴν σκυθρωπὸν καὶ πόσει θυμουμένην; Aeschylus *Libation Bearers* 738 θέτο σκυθρωπὸν ὄμμα). Thus, it should be understood here as pointing to a stern behavior (e.g. Demosthenes 45.68 βαδίζει παρὰ τοὺς τοίχους ἐσκυθρωπακώς), which not only arises from human misfortunes but gloats over them, particularly over a rival's misfortune or ruin. These verses might be spoken by Ino, who begs for

---

[37] For instance, one might think of folk antidotes used against the serpent poison. See McKeown 2017:175–228.

[38] For *pharmaka* in Euripides' work, see Macias 2012, esp. 261–263 for fr. 403 of the *Ino*. On the Hippocratic medicine in tragedy, see Guardasole 2000; Kosak 2004.

Athamas' mercy. Cf. fr. 105a (from the *Alope*) μηδὲ σκυθρωπὸς ἴσθι; fr. 92 (from the *Alcmene*) ἴστω τ' ἄφρων ὢν ὅστις ἄνθρωπος γεγώς / δῆμον κολούει χρήμασιν γαυρούμενος.

Fragment 407

> ἀμουσία τοι μηδ' ἐπ' οἰκτροῖσιν δάκρυ
> στάζειν· κακὸν δέ, χρημάτων ὄντων ἅλις,
> φειδοῖ πονηρᾷ μηδέν' εὖ ποιεῖν βροτῶν

All three verse lines are cited by Stobaeus 3.16.5 (3.481.5 Hense) as exemplary of thrift (περὶ φειδωλίας). But verses 1–2 are also cited by Stobaeus 4.48.20 (5.1013.5 Hense) as explaining that those who suffer misfortunes need support from people sympathizing with their troubles (ὅτι οἱ ἀτυχοῦντες χρῄζουσι τῶν συμπασχόντων); cf. *Helen* 950–951 καίτοι λέγουσιν ὡς πρὸς ἀνδρὸς εὐγενοῦς / ἐν ξυμφοραῖσι δάκρυ' ἀπ' ὀφθαλμῶν βαλεῖν.[39] Deeply considered, fr. 407 labors the content of fr. 406 (suffering along with unfortunate people) by condemning thriftiness, which prevents men from being generous in giving their help. However, what needs to be discussed is the use of the noun ἀμουσία, which is the entry word to this passage. Being compounded of the privative ἀ and the noun μοῦσα, ἀμουσία means absence of music and culture (*Heracles* 676 μὴ ζῴην μετ' ἀμουσίας),[40] something like roughness or rudeness in *Ion* 526 (οὐ φιλῶ φρενοῦν ἀμούσους καὶ μεμηνότας ξένους)[41] and Plato *Sophist* 259e (ἀμούσου τινος καὶ ἀφιλοσόφου); and/or disorder (or discord) in Plato *Laws* 691a (οὐκοῦν δῆλον ὡς πρῶτον τοῦτο οἱ τότε βασιλῆς ἔσχον, τὸ πλεονεκτεῖν τῶν τεθέντων νόμων, καὶ ὃ λόγῳ τε καὶ ὅρκῳ ἐπήνεσαν, οὐ συνεφώνησαν αὐτοῖς, ἀλλὰ ἡ διαφωνία, ὡς ἡμεῖς φαμεν, οὖσα ἀμαθία μεγίστη, δοκοῦσα δὲ σοφία, πάντ' ἐκεῖνα διὰ πλημμέλειαν καὶ ἀμουσίαν τὴν πικρὰν διέφθειρεν;). Continuing her speech to

---

[39] See Waern 1985.

[40] For complete content I give the whole second strophe of the second stasimon: *Heracles* 673–686 οὐ παύσομαι τὰς Χάριτας / ταῖς Μούσαισιν συγκαταμει-/γνύς, ἡδίσταν συζυγίαν. / μὴ ζῴην μετ' ἀμουσίας, / αἰεὶ δ' ἐν στεφάνοισιν εἴην· / ἔτι τοι γέρων ἀοιδὸς / κελαδῶ Μναμοσύναν, / ἔτι τὰν Ἡρακλέους / καλλίνικον ἀείδω / παρά τε Βρόμιον οἰνοδόταν / παρά τε χέλυος ἑπτατόνου / μολπὰν καὶ Λίβυν αὐλόν. / οὔπω καταπαύσομεν / Μούσας αἵ μ' ἐχόρευσαν (Never shall I stop blending the Graces and the Muses! What a delightful pairing they make! I would not have life without the Muses, without garlands always on my head! I may be an aged singer, but still I shall celebrate Memory, still sing of Hercules' glorious victories, to the accompaniment of Bromius, giver of wine, and accompanied by the tunes of the seven-stringed lyre, made of tortoise shell, and by the Libyan pipes. Never shall I restrain the Muses who stirred me to dance. Translation by Waterfield 2003).

[41] Cf. Aristophanes *Wasps* 1074 ῥᾳδίως ἐγὼ διδάξω, κἂν ἄμουσος ᾖ τὸ πρίν.

Athamas, Ino would express her displeasure with him by enumerating negative characteristics of his character.

Fragment 408

> ἐν ἐλπίσιν χρὴ τοὺς σοφοὺς ἔχειν βίον

Fr. 408 is cited by Stobaeus 4.46.3 (5.997.9 Hense) as an example of a saying about hope (περὶ ἐλπίδος).[42] The addressee is rather Ino; the speaker would be Themisto sympathizing with Ino for her situation, or Athamas consoling her.

ἐν ἐλπίσιν: the prepositional adjunct shows the way of dwelling on hope. Cf. Plato *Laws* 718a ἐν ἐλπίσιν ἀγαθαῖς διάγοντες τὸ πλεῖστον τοῦ βίου; pseudo-Lucian Asinus 47 τὸν βίον εἶχον ἐν ἡδονῇ καὶ τρυφῇ.

ἔχειν βίον: ἄγειν βίον Schmidt 1886–1887:1.112; cf. *Cyclops* 453 μόνον δ’ ἔχοντα βίοτον ἡδέως ἄγειν.

Fragment 409

> μήτ’ εὐτυχοῦσα πᾶσαν ἡνίαν χάλα
> κακῶς τε πράσσουσ’ ἐλπίδος κεδνῆς ἔχου.

Fr. 409 is also cited by Stobaeus 4.46.5 (5.998.1 Hense) as a saying about hope (περὶ ἐλπίδος). However, the reference to hope in verse line 2 follows a saying about the importance of measure in happiness in the first verse line, on which perhaps the meaning of the fragment is focused. As Hartung observed, the content of this fragment is relevant to that of fr. 418.[43]

1. πᾶσαν ἡνίαν: For the noun ἡνία (ἡ), *Andromache* 178 δυοῖν γυναικοῖν ἀνδρ’ ἕν’ ἡνίας ἔχειν; Aeschylus *Persians* 193 ἐν ἡνίασί τ’ εἶχεν εὔαρκτον στόμα; Sophocles *Ajax* 847 ἴδῃς, ἐπισχὼν χρυσόνωτον ἡνίαν; Aristophanes *Ecclesiazusae* 466 μὴ παραλαβοῦσαι τῆς πόλεως τὰς ἡνίας, 508 χάλα συναπτοὺς ἡνίας Λακωνικάς; Pindar *Pythian* 5.32 γέρας ἀμφέβαλε τεαῖσιν κόμαις, ἀκηράτοις ἀνίαις. Being an adjunct to ἡνίαν, πᾶσιν makes the meaning of the verb χάλα (to which πᾶσαν ἡνίαν is an object) slacken completely. The addressee is a woman (εὐτυχοῦσα), either Ino or Themisto.

---

[42] Cf. the archaic Greek thought of Hope in Hesiod *Works and Days* 97–98 [Ἐλπὶς] ἔνδον ἔμιμνε πίθου ὑπὸ χείλεσιν, οὐδὲ θύραζε / ἐξέπτη ...

[43] Hartung 1843:1.460.

Fragment 410

> τοιάνδε χρὴ γυναικὶ πρόσπολον ἐᾶν
> ἥτις τὸ μὲν δίκαιον οὐ σιγήσεται,
> τὰ δ᾽ αἰσχρὰ μισεῖ καὶ κατ᾽ ὀφθαλμοὺς ἔχει

Fr. 410 is cited by Stobaeus 4.28.2 (5.677.6 Hense) as a saying about *oikonomia* (Οἰκονομικός). The Greek word οἰκονομία is a compound, composed of the two nouns οἶκος (house) and νόμος (law, custom). Therefore, οἰκονομία literally means household management. In all probability, Stobaeus cites these verse lines as referring to the right of (upper class) women to be allowed or assigned virtuous maids.

1. πρόσπολον: Stobaeus' Greek text is unmetrical at πρόσπολον. Emendations proposed are προσπολεῖν ἐᾶν,[44] in accordance with *The Trojan Women* 264 (τύμβῳ τέτακται προσπολεῖν Ἀχιλλέως) and *Alcestis* 1024 (δίδωμι τήνδε σοῖσι προσπολεῖν δόμοις).[45]

2–3. What is praised as a virtue in a maid is her courage to disclose a secret when right, and express her hate for immoral people despite her low status.

3. ἔχει: Emendations proposed are ἐρεῖ (Dobree, Bergk) according to Aristophanes' *Frogs* 626 (ἵνα σοι κατ᾽ ὀφθαλμοὺς λέγῃ);[46] ψέγει (Schmidt 1886–1887:1.1); κεῖ ... ἔχει (Heath 170, Valckenaer); καὶ ... ἔχει (αἰδοῖ καλύπτραν) (West) with Theognis 579 (ἐχθαίρω κακὸν ἄνδρα, καλυψαμένη δὲ πάρειμι) as an example. The speaker would not be Athamas, but Themisto who would praise the integrity of her unknown servant's (Ino's) character along with her modesty (or courage).

Fragment 411

> ἴστω δὲ μηδεὶς ταῦθ᾽ ἃ σιγᾶσθαι χρεών·
> μικροῦ γὰρ ἐκ λαμπτῆρος Ἰδαῖον λέπας
> πρήσειεν ἄν τις, καὶ πρὸς ἄνδρ᾽ εἰπὼν ἕνα
> πύθοιντ᾽ ἂν ἀστοὶ πάντες {ἃ κρύπτειν χρεών}

All four verse lines are cited by Stobaeus 3.41.1 (3.757.5 Hense) as an example of speaking about secrecy (π. ἀπορρήτων). Verses 2–4 (μικροῦ γὰρ ... πάντες) are cited by Plutarch *De Garrulitate* 10 (507b). Verses 2–3 (μικροῦ γὰρ ... πρήσειεν ἄν τις) are referred to in the Scholia on Pindar *Pythian* 3.66–67 Drachman (2.73.10)

---

[44] Musgrave 1778:2.568; Bergk 1833:32–33; Herwerden 1873–1874:2.109.
[45] See in detail the bibliographic references by Kannicht in TrGF 5.1 *ad loc.*
[46] Cf. *Electra* 910 ἅ γ᾽ εἰπεῖν ἤθελον κατ᾽ ὄμμα σόν; *Rhesus* 421 μέμφομαί σοι καὶ λέγω κατ᾽ ὄμμα σόν; Xenophon *Hieron* 1.14 τυράννου κατ᾽ ὀφθαλμοὺς κατηγορεῖν.

"πολλὰν δ' {ἐν} ὄρει πῦρ ἐξ ἑνὸς / σπέρματος ἐνθορὸν ἄϊστωσεν ὕλαν"· ὥσπερ ἐάν τις εἰς ὕλην πολλὴν σπινθῆρα βάλῃ, ... πᾶσα ἡ ὕλη συγκαίεται ... καὶ Εὐριπίδης· "μικροῦ γὰρ ... πρήσειεν ἄν τις." The speaker may be Themisto, confiding in Ino (whose real identity she does not know) her plot against Athamas' children by Ino.

2. μικροῦ: σμικροῦ is not improbable; cf. fr. 355 (from *Erechtheus*) ναῦς ἡ μεγίστη κρεῖσσον ἢ μικρὸν σκάφος.

Ἰδαῖον λέπας is the name of Zeus' birth place and cult site in Crete or the great mountain south of Troy.[47] For the connection of the Cretan Ida with light (/fire), see fr. 472.1–15 (from the *Cretans*), where there is a chorus' projection to the orgiastic dances of the Corybantes on the mountain Ida in Crete, with special reference to the torches they hold: Διὸς Ἰδαίου μύστης γενόμην / καὶ νυκτιπόλου Ζαγρέως βούτης / τὰς ὠμοφάγους δαῖτας τελέσας / Μητρί τ' ὀρεία δᾶδας ἀνασχὼν / †καὶ Κουρήτων / βάκχος ἐκλήθην ὁσιωθείς. On the other hand, the mount Ida in Troy may be connected with fire only indirectly, through the murderous firebrand Hecuba dreamed of when she was pregnant with Paris. The mythical narrative is known to Pindar *Paeans* fr. 8a.19–23 (... ἔδοξ[ε γάρ / τεκεῖν πυρφόρον ἐρι[/ Ἑκατόγχειρα, σκληρᾷ [/ Ἴλιον πᾶσάν νιν ἐπὶ π[έδον / κατερεῖψαι ...), but the complete story is found in the later mythographic tradition (Apollodorus 3.12.5, Hyginus *Fabula* 91 [*Paris*]) with details of the infant Alexander's exposure on the mount Ida by Priam. In all probability, the dream of Hecuba and the exposure of Alexander/Paris are details of the fifth century tradition, too; at least, they might have been narrated in the prologue of Euripides' *Alexander* (TrGF 5.1.3 iii). Alexander's exposure is explicitly mentioned in the *Iphigenia in Aulis* 1283–1299 and assumed in the *Andromache* 293–300 and *The Trojan Women* 920–922. Nowhere is Ἰδαῖον λέπας directly associated with the firebrand of Hecuba's dream, except for the characterization of Paris as a baleful semblance of a fireband in *The Trojan Women* 922 (δαλοῦ πικρὸν μίμημ', Ἀλέξανδρον τότε) and Ἰδαῖος in the *Iphigenia in Aulis* 1289–1290 (Πάριν, ὃς Ἰδαῖος Ἰ- / δαῖος ἐλέγετ' ἐλέγετ' ἐν Φρυγῶν πόλει).

4. ἃ κρύπτειν χρεών is unmetrical in Stobaeus' text; it is omitted by Plutarch, and deleted by Herwerden 1862:52.[48] Emendations proposed are οὓς κρύπτειν χρεών (Dobree) and ἃ στέγειν χρεών (Enger 1863) in accordance with the Scholia on Sophocles' *Philoctetes* 136 στέγειν: κρύπτειν.

---

[47] Light on mount Ida Crete's highest peak at 2456 meters.
[48] See Wilamowitz 1895:1.52 *ad Heracles* 186.

Fragment 412

> ἐμοὶ γὰρ εἴη πτωχός, εἰ δὲ βούλεται
> πτωχοῦ κακίων, ὅστις ὢν εὔνους ἐμοί
> φόβον παρελθὼν τἀπὸ καρδίας ἐρεῖ

Fr. 412 is quoted by Stobaeus 3.13.12 (3.455.14 Hense) as representative of outspokenness (π. παρρησίας); it is also referred to by Plutarch *De Adulatore et Amico* 22 (63a) as representative of one's devotion to his friend, where it is followed by another quotation, from the *Erechtheus* (fr. 362. 18–20): οὐδεὶς γάρ ἐστι ῥᾳδίως πλούσιος οὐδὲ βασιλεὺς οἷος εἰπεῖν "ἐμοὶ γὰρ εἴη–ἐρεῖ," ἀλλ᾽ ὥσπερ οἱ τραγῳδοὶ χοροῦ δέονται φίλων συναδόντων ἢ θεάτρου συνεπικροτοῦντος. ὅθεν "φίλους δὲ τοὺς μὲν μὴ χαλῶντας ἐν λόγοις / κέκτησο· τοὺς δὲ πρὸς χάριν σὺν ἡδονῇ / τῇ σῇ †πονηροὺς† κλῇθρον εἰργέτω στέγης"). The passage from the *Erechtheus* is also cited by Stobaeus 3.14.3 (3.469.4 Hense), but as a paradigm of flattery (π. κολακείας).

In fr. 412, what is praised is a friend's devotion and honesty, which are considered to be opposite to wealth and go together with poverty.

1. The adjective πτωχός means a poor beggar man. It is further exalted in the following verses (2–3), where the crucial terms of pure friendship are developed.

2. πτωχοῦ κακίων: the comparative κακίων, joined with πτωχοῦ, expresses utter poverty.

εὔνους: compound with the adverb εὖ (well) and the noun νόος (mind), the epithet characterizes a man who is high in someone else's favor (/good graces).

3. παρελθών means παρείς (LSJ s.v. παρέρχομαι [4]); being joined with φόβον, παρελθών here is said for someone who gets over fear.

τἀπὸ καρδίας ἐρεῖ (heartfelt words, words coming from the heart): it is rather a proverbial phrase, typical of speaking in all sincerity and honesty. Cf. *Iphigenia in Aulis* 475 ἐρεῖν σοι τἀπὸ καρδίας σαφῶς; Plutarch *De Sollertia Animalium* 7 (964c) ταῦτα μὲν, ὦ φίλε, "τἀπὸ καρδίας" τῶν ἀνδρῶν ἐξείρηκας, where τἀπὸ καρδίας does not characterize the speech of the speaker himself, but that of another person(s).

In all probability, the speaker is Themisto, who praises the devotion, courage, and honesty of her new confidant maid, the poor Ino.

Fragment 413

> ἐπίσταμαι δὲ πάνθ᾽ ὅσ᾽ εὐγενῆ χρεών,
> σιγᾶν θ᾽ ὅπου δεῖ καὶ λέγειν ἵν᾽ ἀσφαλές,
> ὁρᾶν θ᾽ ἃ δεῖ με κοὐχ ὁρᾶν ἃ μὴ πρέπει,

γαστρὸς κρατεῖν δέ· καὶ γὰρ ἐν κακοῖσιν ὢν
ἐλευθέροισιν ἐμπεπαίδευμαι τρόποις

All five verses are cited by Stobaeus 4.29.62 (5.728.5 Hense) as featuring a noble man's behavior (ὁποῖον χρὴ εἶναι τὸν εὐγενῆ). Verses 1–3 are cited by Orion *Florilegium* 1.5. Verses 1–2 are cited by Plutarch (1) *De Garrulitate* 9 (506c), attributing the words to Euripides' Ino, who is presented to speak with paradigmatic outspokenness: ἡ δ' Εὐριπίδειος Ἰνὼ παρρησίαν ἄγουσα περὶ αὑτῆς εἰδέναι φησί "σιγᾶν θ'-ἀσφαλές·" οἱ γὰρ εὐγενοῦς καὶ βασιλικῆς τῷ ὄντι παιδείας τυχόντες πρῶτον σιγᾶν, εἶτα λαλεῖν μανθάνουσιν. Verse line 2 is frequently cited or paraphrased; for example, Plutarch (2) *De Exilio* 16 (606a) … καὶ σιωπῆς δεομένοις, ὥσπερ αὐτὸς [Εὐριπίδης] βέλτιον εἴρηκε "σιγᾶν θ'-ἀσφαλές" and Gellius *Attic Nights* 13.19.4 *id quoque animadvertimus aput Aeschylum* ἐν τῷ πυρφόρῳ Προμηθεῖ *et aput Euripidem in tragoedia quae inscripta est* Ἰνώ, *eundem esse versum absque paucis syllabis. Aeschylus sic:* "σιγῶν θ' ὅπου δεῖ καὶ λέγων τὰ καίρια," *Euripides ita:* "σιγᾶν θ'-ἀσφαλές," where the parallelism of the *Ino*'s "σιγᾶν θ'-ἀσφαλές" with an almost identical verse line from the fragmentary Aeschylus' *Prometheus Pyrphorus* (TrGF 3 F 208) is remarkable.[49] At verse line 4, the fact that ὤν, a (singular) masculine participle, refers to Ino is problematic; probably, the masculine word is due to the fact that Ino's view here is part of an opinion on her nobility as an individual, for which see *Helen* 1630 δοῦλος ὤν.

Ino's position as Themisto's servant would not have had the characteristics of subjugation, but of loyal servitude, as it usually occurs in the role of a nurse in ancient tragedy. Examples come from the *Medea* and *Hippolytus*, at least. In the prologue of the *Medea*, the Nurse feels great grief because she sees that the affairs of her mistress, Medea, are very grave; inside the palace she (the nurse) remains silent; but, since her sorrow and anxiety are very great, she comes out in order to speak aloud her mistress's troubles to the earth and the sky (54–58 χρηστοῖσι δούλοις ξυμφορὰ τὰ δεσποτῶν / κακῶς πίτνοντα καὶ φρενῶν ἀνθάπτεται. / ἐγὼ γὰρ ἐς τοῦτ' ἐκβέβηκ' ἀλγηδόνος / ὥσθ' ἵμερός μ' ὑπῆλθε γῇ τε κοὐρανῷ / λέξαι μολούσῃ δεῦρο δεσποίνης τύχας [To trusty servants it is a disaster when the dice of their masters' fortunes fall badly; it touches their hearts. So great is the grief I feel that the desire stole over me to come out here and speak my mistress's troubles to the earth and the sky]). And when the Tutor, who has arrived with the children, speaks about Medea's latest trouble, unknown to her, the Nurse begs him not to keep it from her and promises silence (65–66 μή, πρὸς γενείου, κρύπτε σύνδουλον σέθεν· / σιγὴν γάρ, εἰ χρή, τῶνδε θήσομαι πέρι [I beg you by your beard, do not conceal this from your fellow-slave! I will keep it a secret if I

---

[49]   See further the detailed bibliographic references by Kannicht TrGF 5.1 *ad loc.*

must] Translation by Kovacs 1994). On the other hand, moderation is one of her own maxims for Phaedra's nurse in the *Hippolytus*: she wishes the rule of moderation could apply to friendship (253–257), expresses her disapproval of life's strict unswerving practices (261), and offers her open approval of moderation (262–266). She has less praise for extremes than for nothing in excess (264–265 οὕτω τὸ λίαν ἧσσον ἐπαινῶ / τοῦ μηδὲν ἄγαν).

The dramatic condition itself of the Eurpidean Ino as Themisto's servant is a special one. Due to her mythic background (a daughter of the king Cadmus), Ino would have nobility written on her face.[50] Thus, she could express noble ideas in accordance with her inherited nobility (*eugeneia*), approving balance and moderation (silence, tactfulness) and disapproving life's excessive practices (outspokenness, gluttony). Certainly, her humble appearance on stage would be provocative for the aristocratic belief in inherited nobility;[51] being disguised as a humble tragic heroine, the noble born Ino, who expresses noble ideas, is herself a challenge to the training of the aristocratic nobility. Direct challenge of inherited nobility is the crucial element in the dramatic synthesis of the surviving *Electra* (performed later than the *Ino*) where the title heroine, a daughter of Agamemnon, is dramatically deprived from her inherited nobility by being given in marriage to a farmer. For such a manipulation by Euripides, the sophists' new criticism of the aristocratic belief is a possible influence. Thus, in our fragment, the emphasis on the value of moderate silence may also have social and political connotations. Especially, Ino's silence about Themisto's secret plan does not have any ethical connection with the wife's glory in her household or with female glory in the city of Athens, praised in Thucydides (2.45.2) by Pericles. Cf. *The Trojan Women* 646–655, where the captive Andromache appears to express traditional ideas, but her thinking is rather with the new (particularly, 650 τούτου [τοῦ οὐκ ἔνδον μένειν] παρεῖσα πόθον ἔμιμνον ἐν δόμοις). However, Ino's *sententiae* against gluttony, which characterizes mostly ignoble behavior and people of a low level,[52] might be a special expression of her maenadic

---

[50] See *Ion* 237–240, where the title hero understands from her face that the unknown Creousa has a noble birth: γενναιότης σοι καὶ τρόπων τεκμήριον / τὸ σχῆμ' ἔχεις τόδ', ἥτις εἶ ποτ', ὦ γύναι. / γνοίη δ' ἂν ὡς τὰ πολλά γ' ἀνθρώπου πέρι / τὸ σχῆμ' ἰδών τις εἰ πέφυκεν εὐγενής (There is nobility in you, and you have an appearance that is a witness to your character, lady, whoever you are. For most men at least, you would know from their appearance if they are well-born. Translation by D. H. Roberts, in Slavitt and Bovie 1998).

[51] The belief in inherited nobility is best conveyed in Pindar's epinician odes (e.g. *Olympian* 9, *Nemean* 3); see Rose 1995:160–161.

[52] Gluttony, as a dramatic characteristic, belongs to satyric drama (e.g. the behavior of Heracles as a satyric hero in the *Alcestis*, which was presented in the position of a satyr play) and comedy. It is remarkable that a series of comments *ad loc.* (Matthiae 1829, Pflugk 1831, Bothe 1844, Meineke 1823, Webster 1967:99) think that verses 4–5 are alien to be spoken by Ino.

abstinence from material pleasures, for which the maenadic physical life in the remote climbs of Cithaeron in Euripides' *Bacchae* (38, 683–711) is paradigmatic.[53]

Fragment 414

> φειδώμεθ' ἀνδρῶν εὐγενῶν, φειδώμεθα,
> κακοὺς δ' ἀποπτύωμεν, ὥσπερ ἄξιοι

Fr. 414 is cited by Stobaeus 4.29.8 (5.705.5 Hense) with the explanation that noblemen are those who live with *arete* (4.29.8 ὅτι εὐγενεῖς οἱ κατ' ἀρετὴν ζῶντες). The explanation is implied by the fragmentary text itself through the hortatory subjunctive of the (double) φειδώμεθα and ἀποπτύωμεν, the object of which are εὐγενῶν and κακούς, respectively. Since then *kakia* is presented as an opposite to nobility, the latter could not but be identified with *arete*, the opposite of *kakia*. In this way, *arete* appears to be the criterion of nobility, and not nobility the precondition for *arete*. Deeply considered, the idea is not necessarily aristocratic, because it connects nobility with human behavior and not aristocratic birth. At any rate, *kakia* here should not be considered a feature of poverty, which is incompatible with Athamas' noble birth. For *kakos* as featuring poverty, see Homer *Odyssey* 4.63–64 (ἀλλ' ἀνδρῶν γένος ἐστὲ διοτρεφέων βασιλήων / σκηπτούχων, ἐπεὶ οὔ κε κακοὶ τοιούσδε τέκοιεν); Sophocles *Oedipus Tyrannus* 1062–1063 (θάρσει· σὺ μὲν γὰρ οὐδ' ἐὰν τρίτης ἐγὼ / μητρὸς φανῶ τρίδουλος, ἐκφανῇ κακή), 1397 (νῦν γὰρ κακός τ' ὢν κἀκ κακῶν εὑρίσκομαι).

1–2. φειδώμεθ'(α) ... φειδώμεθα ... ἀποπτύωμεν: For the urgency of repetition cf. *Heracleidae* 307 δότ', ὦ τέκν', αὐτοῖς χεῖραν δεξιάν, δότε; *Hippolytus* 327 κάκ' ὦ τάλαινά σοι τάδ', εἰ πεύσῃ, κακά (and Barrett 1964); fr. 548.1 νοῦν χρὴ θεᾶσθαι, νοῦν· ...

2. ὥσπερ ἄξιοι: Cf. *Alcestis* 735–736 ἄπαιδε παιδὸς ὄντος, ὥσπερ ἄξιοι, γηράσκετε ... ; *Bacchae* 796 θύσω, φόνον γε θῆλυν, ὥσπερ ἄξιαι.

Fragment 415

> ἄνασσα, πολλοῖς ἔστιν ἀνθρώπων κακά,
> τοῖς δ' ἄρτι λήγει, τοῖς δὲ κίνδυνος μολεῖν.
> κύκλος γὰρ αὐτὸς καρπίμοις τε γῆς φυτοῖς

---

[53] In his *Birth of Tragedy* (Chapter 2), Nietzsche (1873) interpreted the first messenger's descriptions in the *Bacchae* (683–711) as the happiest state of humans, which, keeping them away from materialistic pleasures, expresses their reconciliation with nature and can be attained only in the world of Dionysus.

4   θνητῶν τε γενεᾷ· τῶν μὲν αὔξεται βίος,
        τῶν δὲ φθίνει τε καὶ θερίζεται πάλιν

All five verse lines are cited by Stobaeus 4.41.19 (5.933.5 Hense) as a mediation on the fluidity (and/or mutability) of human happiness (and/or wealth) (ὅτι ἀβέβαιος ἡ τῶν ἀνθρώπων εὐπραξία). Verses 3–5 are cited by Plutarch *Consolatio ad Apollonium* 6 (104b); they are preceded by one more quotation from the *Ino* (fr. 420.2–3; see below) and followed by a quotation from Pindar (*Pythian* 8.95–97 σκιᾶς ὄναρ / ἄνθρωπος. ἀλλ᾽ ὅταν αἴγλα διόσδοτος ἔλθῃ, / λαμπρὸν φέγγος ἔπεστιν ἀνδρῶν καὶ μείλιχος αἰών). Similar ideas are found in the *Danae*, where the features of human τύχη are paralleled to those of aether (fr. 330): ἐς ταὐτὸν ἥκειν φημὶ τὰς βροτῶν τύχας / τῷδ᾽, ὃν καλοῦσιν αἰθέρ᾽, † ᾧ τάδ᾽ ἔστι δή. / οὗτος θέρους τε λαμπρὸν ἐκλάμπει σέλας, / χειμῶνά τ᾽ αὔξει συντιθεὶς πυκνὸν νέφος, / θάλλειν τε καὶ μή, ζῆν τε καὶ φθίνειν ποιεῖ. / οὕτω δὲ θνητῶν σπέρμα· τῶν μὲν εὐτυχεῖ / λαμπρᾷ γαλήνῃ, τῶν δὲ συννέφει πάλιν, / ζῶσίν τε σὺν κακοῖσιν, οἱ δ᾽ / ὄλβου μέτα / φθίνουσ᾽ ἐτείοις προσφερεῖς μεταλλαγαῖς. In Euripides they are rather a *locus communis*. See fr. 518 (from the *Meleagrus*) καὶ κτῆμα δ᾽, ὦ τεκοῦσα, κάλλιστον τόδε, / πλούτου δὲ κρεῖσσον· τοῦ μὲν ὠκεῖα πτέρυξ, / παῖδες δὲ χρηστοί, κἂν θάνωσι, δώμασιν / καλόν τι θησαύρισμα τοῖς τεκοῦσί τε / ἀνάθημα βιότου, κοὔποτ᾽ ἐκλείπει δόμους; *Heracles* 509–512 ... καί μ᾽ ἀφείλεθ᾽ ἡ τύχη / ὥσπερ πτερὸν πρὸς αἰθέρ᾽ ἡμέρᾳ μιᾷ. / ὁ δ᾽ ὄλβος ὁ μέγας ἥ τε δόξ᾽ οὐκ οἶδ᾽ ὅτῳ / βέβαιός ἐστι; *The Trojan Women* 1203–1206 θνητῶν δὲ μῶρος ὅστις εὖ πράσσειν δοκῶν / βέβαια χαίρει· τοῖς τρόποις γὰρ αἱ τύχαι, / ἔμπληκτος ὡς ἄνθρωπος, / ἄλλοτ᾽ ἄλλοσε / πηδῶσι, †κοὐδεὶς αὐτὸς εὐτυχεῖ ποτε†; *Electra* 941–944 ἡ γὰρ φύσις βέβαιος, οὐ τὰ χρήματα. / ἡ μὲν γὰρ αἰεὶ παραμένουσ᾽ αἴρει κακά· / ὁ δ᾽ ὄλβος ἀδίκως καὶ μετὰ σκαιῶν ξυνὼν / ἐξέπτατ᾽ οἴκων, μικρὸν ἀνθήσας χρόνον (and Cropp 1988 *ad loc.*); *Orestes* 340–344 ὁ μέγας ὄλβος οὐ μόνιμος ἐν βροτοῖς· / ἀνὰ δὲ λαῖφος ὥς τις ἀκάτου θοᾶς / τινάξας δαίμων κατέκλυσεν δεινῶν / πόνων ὡς πόντου λάβροις ὀλεθρίοι- / σιν ἐν κύμασιν. Cf. Sophocles *Oedipus Tyrannus* 1282–1284 ὁ πρὶν παλαιὸς δ᾽ ὄλβος ἦν πάροιθε μὲν / ὄλβος δικαίως, νῦν δὲ τῇδε θἠμέρᾳ / στεναγμός, ἄτη, θάνατος, αἰσχύνη ... and TrGF 4 F 591 (from the *Tereus*) ἓν φῦλον ἀνθρώπων, μί᾽ ἔδειξε πατρὸς / καὶ ματρὸς ἡμᾶς ἀμέρα τοὺς πάντας· / οὐδεὶς / ἔξοχος ἄλλος ἔβλαστεν ἄλλου. βόσκει δὲ τοὺς μὲν μοῖρα δυσαμερίας, / τοὺς δὲ δουλεί- / ας ζυγὸν ἔσχεν ἀνάγκας; Homer *Odyssey* 4.236–237 ... ἀτὰρ θεὸς ἄλλοτε ἄλλῳ / Ζεὺς ἀγαθόν τε κακόν τε διδοῖ· δύναται γὰρ ἅπαντα; Archilochus fr. 13.7–9 West ἄλλοτε ἄλλος ἔχει τόδε· νῦν μὲν ἐς ἡμέας / ἐτράπεθ᾽, αἱματόεν δ᾽ ἕλκος ἀναστένομεν, / ἐξαῦτις δ᾽ ἑτέρους ἐπαμείψεται. For the idea of mutability of human affairs, see Krause 1976.

    1. ἄνασσα: a vocative, addressing, most probably, Themisto.

5. θερίζεται: cf. fr. 757.925 (from the *Hypsipyle*) βίον θερίζειν ὥστε κάρπιμον στάχυν.

Fragment 416

> πολλοί γε θνητῶν τῷ θράσει τὰς συμφοράς
> ζητοῦσ' ἀμαυροῦν κἀποκρύπτεσθαι κακά

Fr. 416 is cited by Stobaeus 3.4.9 (3.221.4 Hense) as a paradigm of folly and stupidity (περὶ ἀφροσύνης). It paradoxically reverses a usual *sententia* about the necessity of concealing human misfortunes (ὅτι δεῖ ... τὰς ἀτυχίας κρύπτειν), also found in Stobaeus 4.45.7 (5.994.16 Hense), quoting fr. 460 (from the *Cretan Women*): λύπη μὲν ἄτη περιπεσεῖν αἰσχρᾷ τινι· / εἰ δ' οὖν γένοιτο, / χρὴ περιστεῖλαι καλῶς / κρύπτοντα καὶ μὴ πᾶσι κηρύσσειν τάδε· / γέλως γὰρ ἐχθροῖς γίγνεται τὰ τοιάδε. Cf. also fr. 553 (from the *Oedipus*): ἐκμαρτυρεῖν γὰρ ἄνδρα τὰς αὐτοῦ τύχας / εἰς πάντας ἀμαθές, τὸ δ' ἐπικρύπτεσθαι σοφόν (It is stupid for a man to testify to his misfortunes in front of everybody; concealing them is wise. Translation by Collard, in Collard, Cropp, and Kee 2004). Being the only person who knew Athamas' real situation, Ino could be the speaker of fr. 416, pointing subtly to Athamas' folly, who was in fact unhappy with his polygamy (Themisto instead of Ino), and tried to heal his suffering by hiding it even from himself. Ino's secret service to Themisto was a female psychological bomb that did not take long to explode.

Fragment 417

> κέκτησο δ' ὀρθῶς ἂν ἔχης ἄνευ ψόγου
> † καὶ σμικρὰ σώζων τοὐνεχ' ὃν σέβειν πρέπει †
> μηδ' ὡς κακὸς ναύκληρος, εὖ πράξας ποτέ
> 4 ζητῶν τὰ πλείον', εἶτα πάντ' ἀπώλεσεν

Fr. 417 is cited by Stobaeus (1) 4.31.102 (5.770.5 Hense) as a saying about wealth (π. πλούτου iv. ὅτι τὰ χρήματα ἀβλαβῆ συμμέτρως καὶ δικαίως πορισθέντα ...); verses 1–2 are cited by Stobaeus (2) 3.9.2 (3.346.16 Hense) as a saying about justice (π. δικαιοσύνης). Kannicht comments that each quotation proceeds from a different *sententia* ("alterutra scriptura ex alia sententia irrepsisse videtur").

1. Cf. fr. 362.11–13 (from the *Erechtheus*): ἀδίκως δὲ μὴ κτῶ χρήματ', ἢν βούλῃ πολὺν / χρόνον μελάθροις ἐμμένειν· τὰ γὰρ κακῶς / οἴκους ἐσελθόντ' οὐκ ἔχει σωτηρίαν (Do not acquire possessions unjustly if you want them to remain a long time in your dwelling; those that enter a house wrongly do not have permanence. Translation by Cropp, in Collard, Cropp, and Kee 1995).

4. τὰ πλείονα is compared with what is meant to be an object to εὖ πράξας; cf. fr. 822b.15 κρύπτω] τὰ πλείω, πόλλ' ἔχων εἰπεῖν ἔπη (from the *Phrixus*).

Fragment 418

> Γίγνωσκε τἀνθρώπεια μηδ' ὑπερμέτρως
> ἄλγει· κακοῖς γὰρ οὐ σὺ πρόσκεισαι μόνη

Fr. 418 is cited by Stobaeus 4.56.7 (5.1125.3 Hense) as an example of consolation (παρηγορικά). The main consolation argument (you are not the only person lying in misfortunes) is also found in *Hippolytus* 834 (ΧΟ.) οὐ σοὶ τάδ', ὦναξ, ἦλθε δὴ μόνῳ κακά; *Medea* 1017–1018 οὔτοι μόνη σὺ σῶν ἀπεζύγης τέκνων· / κούφως φέρειν χρὴ θνητὸν ὄντα συμφοράς; *Helen* 464 πολλοὶ κακῶς πράσσουσιν, οὐ σὺ δὴ μόνος. The consolation is worded in the imperative mood γίγνωσκε (understand) and μηδ' ... ἄλγει (do not pain/grieve), to which the adverb ὑπερμέτρως (beyond measure/to excess) is attached.

2. πρόσκεισαι here means lie near something or somebody; cf. Sophocles *Antigone* 1223 τὸν δ' ἀμφὶ μέσσῃ περιπετῆ προσκείμενον (for Haemon embracing the dead Antigone with his arms thrown around her waist). From the feminine adjective μόνη we easily understand that the addressee should be a woman, Ino in all probability. To be exact, it has been supposed that the speaker is the leader of the women's chorus of the play, who addresses the *flebilis* Ino in iambic trimeter (Valckenaer 1767:179).[54] But Themisto would not be excluded either as an addressee or a speaker; in that case, the fragment would belong to a dialogic scene between her and her servant (Ino), arguing and plotting against Athamas. Hartung (1.460) connected this fragment with fr. 409. In a fragment from the *Dictys*, where the title hero tries to console the miserable Danae, the consolation argument is developed through some examples of human misfortunes (fr. 332):[55] δοκεῖς τὸν Ἅιδην σῶν τι φροντίζειν γόων / καὶ παῖδ' ἀνήσειν τὸν σόν, εἰ θέλεις στένειν; / παῦσαι· βλέπουσα δ' εἰς τὰ τῶν πέλας κακά / ῥᾴων γένοιτ' ἄν, εἰ λογίζεσθαι θέλοις, / ὅσοι τε δεσμοῖς ἐκμεμόχθηνται βροτῶν / ὅσοι τε γηράσκουσιν ὀρφανοὶ τέκνων / τούς τ' ἐκ μέγιστον ὀλβίας τυραννίδος / τὸ μηδὲν ὄντας· ταῦτά σε σκοπεῖν χρεών (Do you think that Hades is concerned at all for your laments, and will send your son back up if you will go on grieving? Stop! You'd feel easier if you looked at the troubles of those near at hand, if you'd be willing to consider how many of mankind have been exhausted by struggling

---

[54] *Flebilis* is the characterization of Ino by Horace, which is contracted to Medea's ferocity (*De Arte Poetica* 123 *sit Medea ferox invictaque, flebilis Ino*); see Brink 1971 *ad loc*. According to Webster 1967:98, "it suits the oppressed Ino" of Euripides' story. In my opinion, it could reflect generally Ino's oppressed situation in Athamas' home after her return from Cithaeron.

[55] See Karamanou 2006 *ad loc*.

with bonds, how many grow bereft of children and those who are nothing after ruling in the greatest prosperity: these are the things you should contemplate. Translation by Collard and Cropp 2008a).

Fragment 419

> βίᾳ νυν ἕλκετ' ὦ κακοὶ τιμὰς βροτοί,
> καὶ κτᾶσθε πλοῦτον παντόθεν θηρώμενοι,
> σύμμεικτα μὴ δίκαια καὶ δίκαι' ὁμοῦ·
> 4 ἔπειτ' ἀμᾶσθε τῶνδε δύστηνον θέρος

Fr. 419 is cited by Stobaeus (1) 3.10.23 (3.413.8 Hense) as a saying about injustice and avarice (π. ἀδικίας καὶ φιλαργυρίας ...).[56] It is also cited by Stobaeus (2) 4.31.56 (5.755.1 Hense) as an aphorism of wealth (ψόγος πλούτου). All four verses may be uttered either in indicative or in imperative mood (*paraenetici*; see Stevens *ad Andromache* 622–623), referring (in both cases) to universal humankind and not to a particular dramatic person; cf. *Suppliants* 949–951 ... ὦ ταλαίπωροι βροτῶν, / τί κτᾶσθε λόγχας καὶ κατ' ἀλλήλων φόνους / τίθεσθε; παύσασθ' ...).[57] Aphorisms of wealth are found elsewhere in Euripides: *Heracles* 774–776 (ὁ χρυσὸς ἅ τ' εὐτυχία / φρενῶν βροτοὺς ἐξάγεται / δύνασιν ἄδικον ἐφέλκων), in the chorus' third stasimon referring to the gods as protecting justice against injustice; *Alexandros* fr. 54 (κακόν τι παίδευμ' ἦν ἄρ' εἰς εὐανδρίαν / ὁ πλοῦτος ἀνθρώποισιν αἵ τ' ἄγαν τρυφαί· / πενία δὲ δύστηνον μέν, ἀλλ' ὅμως τρέφει / μοχθεῖν τ' ἀμείνω τέκνα καὶ δραστήρια) and fr. 55 (ἄδικον ὁ πλοῦτος, πολλὰ δ' οὐκ ὀρθῶς ποιεῖ); *Erechtheus* fr. 354 (τὰς οὐσίας γὰρ μᾶλλον ἢ τὰς ἁρπαγάς / τιμᾶν δίκαιον· οὔτε γὰρ πλοῦτός ποτε / βέβαιος ἄδικος); *Phaethon* fr. 776 (δεινόν γε· τοῖς πλουτοῦσι τοῦτο δ' ἔμφυτον / σκαιοῖσιν εἶναι· τί ποτε τοῦτο ταἴτιον; / ἆρ' ὄλβος αὐτοῖς ὅτι τυφλὸς συνηρεφεῖ / τυφλὰς ἔχουσι τὰς φρένας καὶ τῆς τύχης;). On the other hand, poverty was rejected, too, as something that is shameful. See *Electra* 375–376 ... ἀλλ' ἔχει νόσον / πενία, διδάσκει δ' ἄνδρα τῇ χρείᾳ κακόν; Aeschines 1.88 ἐκεῖνοι μέν γε οἱ ταλαίπωροι οὐ δυνάμενοι γῆρας ἅμα καὶ πενίαν ἀμύνεσθαι, τὰ μέγιστα τῶν ἐν ἀνθρώποις κακῶν ...[58]

3. σύμμεικτα: mixed. See fr. 472a (from the *Cretans*) σύμμικτον εἶδος κἀποφώλιον βρέφος (for Minotaurus); Sophocles *Ajax* 53–54 καὶ πρός τε ποίμνας ἐκτρέπω σύμμεικτά τε / λείας ἄδαστα βουκόλων φρουρήματα; Hesiod *Works and Days* 563 γῆ πάντων μήτηρ καρπὸν σύμμικτον ἐνείκῃ; Lysias 19.27

---

[56] Cf. fr. 297 from the *Bellerephontes*, speaking about human malice: ὡς ἔμφυτος μὲν πᾶσιν ἀνθρώποις κάκη. / ὅστις δὲ πλεῖστον μισθὸν εἰς χεῖρας λαβών / κακὸς γένηται, τῷδε συγγνώμη μὲν οὔ· / πλείω δὲ μισθὸν μείζονος τόλμης ἔχων / τὸν τῶν λεγόντων ῥᾷον ἂν φέροι ψόγον.

[57] Schadewaldt 1926:129.

[58] Karamanou 2017:222–224, 276–277.

χαλκώματα δὲ σύμμεικτα; Herodotus 7.55.2 ἡγέοντο δὲ πρῶτα μὲν οἱ μύριοι Πέρσαι ἐστεφανωμένοι πάντες, μετὰ δὲ τούτους ὁ σύμμεικτος στρατὸς παντοίων ἐθνέων; Thucydides 6.4.6 καὶ τὴν πόλιν αὐτὸς ξυμμείκτων ἀνθρώπων οἰκίσας.

4. ἀμᾶσθε: the verb ἀμάω (usually used as ἀμῶμαι) means reap and, meta-phorically, misappropriate, embezzle. See Hesiod *Theogony* 599 ἀλλότριον κάματον σφετέρην ἐς γαστέρ' ἀμῶνται (for those who misappropriate the toil of others or convert the funds of others to their own use).

Fragment 420

> ὁρᾷς τυράννους διὰ μακρῶν ηὐξημένους
> ὡς μικρὰ τὰ σφάλλοντα, καὶ μί' ἡμέρα
> τὰ μὲν καθεῖλεν ὑψόθεν, τὰ δ' ἦρ' ἄνω.
>
> 4   ὑπόπτερος δ' ὁ πλοῦτος· οἷς γὰρ ἦν ποτε,
> ἐξ ἐλπίδων πίπτοντας ὑπτίους ὁρῶ

Fr. 420 is cited by Stobaeus 4.41.1 (5.927.4 Hense) as a saying about the muta-bility of wealth (ὅτι ἀβέβαιος ...). According to the narrative in Philostratus *Vita Apollonii* 7.5, these iambic trimeters could have been told towards the end of the play. Their content concerns instability of human affairs, a *locus communis* in Greek culture.[59] Verses 1–2 and 4–5 are preserved badly damaged in the *Papyrus Cairo* 65445 (third century BCE).[60] Verses 1–2 are quoted by Demetrius Phalereus FrGHist 228 fr. 24; Plutarch *Consolatio ad Apollonium* 6 (104 a) μικρότατα–ἦρ' ἄνω; Philo Judaeus *De somniis* 1.154 (3.237.21 Wendland) ἡ μία ἡμέρα τὸν μὲν–ἦρεν ἄνω; Johannes Lydus *De mensibus* 4.7 ἐν μιᾷ ἡμέρᾳ τὸν μὲν–ἦρ' ἄνω. Verses 1–3 are cited by Philostratus *Vita Apollonii* 7.5 with a significant reference to a later performance of Euripides' *Ino*: τραγῳδίας δὲ ὑποκριτοῦ παρελθόντος ἐς τὴν Ἔφεσον ἐπὶ τῇ Ἰνοῖ τῷ δράματι, καὶ ἀκροωμένου τοῦ τῆς Ἀσίας ἄρχοντος ..., ὁ μὲν ὑποκριτὴς ἐπέραινεν ἤδη τὰ ἰαμβεῖα, ἐν οἷς ὁ Εὐριπίδης "διὰ μακρῶν αὐξηθέντας τοὺς τυράννους ἁλίσκεσθαι" φησίν "ὑπὸ μικρῶν," ἀναπηδήσας δὲ ὁ Ἀπολλώνιος "ἀλλ' ὁ δειλός," ἔφη, "οὗτος οὔτε Εὐριπίδου ξυνίησιν οὔτε ἐμοῦ." From the masculine epithet δειλός we can understand that the dramatic person (impersonated by the actor) is male; but the characterization of cowardice refers only to the actor, because it is voiced in a later performance of the *Ino* by a disgruntled spectator who breaks the theatrical illusion by even evoking Euripides himself.

4. ὑπόπτερος means winged/feathered. See fr. 518.2 (from the *Meleagrus*) πλούτου δὲ κρεῖσσον· τοῦ μὲν ὠκεῖα πτέρυξ; *Electra* 943–944 ὁ δ' ὄλβος ἀδίκως

---

[59] See the quotations by Kannicht (TrGF 5.1) *ad loc.*
[60] Guéraud and Jouguet 1938:4/16.126–129 (Pack 1965:26–42).

καὶ μετὰ σκαιῶν ξυνὼν / ἐξέπτατ' οἴκων, σμικρὸν ἀνθήσας χρόνον; *Hecuba* 1264 ὑποπτέροις νώτοισιν ἢ ποίῳ τρόπῳ(;); *Helen* 1236 μεθίημι νεῖκος τὸ σόν, ἴτω δ' ὑπόπτερον; Aeschylus *Libation Bearers* 602–603 ἴστω δ', ὅστις οὐχ ὑπόπτερος / φροντίσιν; Sophocles *Philoctetes* 288–289 τόξον τόδ' ἐξηύρισκε, τὰς ὑποπτέρους / βάλλον πελείας ... ; Mimnermus 12.7 χρυσοῦ τιμήεντος, ὑπόπτερος, ἄκρον ἐφ' ὕδωρ; Pindar *Olympian* 9.24 θᾶσσον καὶ ναὸς ὑποπτέρου παντᾷ; *Pythian* 8.90–91 ἐξ ἐλπίδος πέταται / ὑποπτέροις ἀνορέαις; Herodotus 3.107.2 ὄφιες ὑπόπτεροι.

5. ὑπτίους means overturned, upset, inverted. See Aeschylus *Seven Against Thebes* 459 ἐξ ὑπτίου 'πήδησεν εὐχάλκου κράνους; *Suppliant Women* 96–98 ἰάπτει δ' ἐλπίδων / ἀφ' ὑψιπύργων πανώλεις βροτούς; Sophocles *Antigone* 716–717 ... ὑπτίοις κάτω / στρέψας τὸ λοιπὸν σέλμασιν ναυτίλλεται; Aristophanes *Lysistrata* 185 θὲς ἐς τὸ πρόσθεν ὑπτίαν τὴν ἀσπίδα; Herodotus 4.72.3 ἀψῖδος δὲ ἥμισυ ἐπὶ δύο ξύλα στήσαντες ὕπτιον; Thucydides 7.82.3 καὶ τὸ ἀργύριον ὃ εἶχον ἅπαν κατέθεσαν ἐσβαλόντες ἐς ἀσπίδας ὑπτίας, καὶ ἐνέπλησαν ἀσπίδας τέσσαρας.

Fragment 421

κοίλοις ἐν ἄντροις ἄλυχνος, ὥστε θήρ, μόνος

Fr. 421 is cited by Pollux 7.178 (2.100.27 Bethe) as a paradigm of words deriving from λύχνος. This verse is usually attributed to Athamas, who deplores his own condition (probably his helpless imprisonment in a dark cave) after having killed his son Learchus.[61] But the speaker could also be Ino who either damns Athamas and wishes for his exile to wild places,[62] or prepares for her own exodus (suicide) to escape to the solitude of the darkness of Hades. In that case, we must eliminate the comma after the noun θήρ, which should be modified by the adjective μόνος: κοίλοις ἐν ἄντροις ἄλυχνος, ὥστε θὴρ μόνος. Finglass does not doubt that the fragment describes Athamas, but places it in a *deus ex machina* scene at the end of the play.[63]

ἄλυχνος: someone who wants for a lamp (who lives without a lamp). The epithet is found in Diogenes Laertius 1.81 enumerating nicknames given by Alceus to Pittacus (ἀλλὰ μὴν καὶ ζοφοδορπίδαν ὡς ἄλυχνον), who dined in the dark because he dispensed with a lamp.

---

[61] Valckenaer 1767:180; Seaford 1990:86; Collard and Cropp 2008b:459.
[62] Cf. Apollodorus *Library* 1.9.2, where, at the end of his adventures, the exile Athamas builds his own country, the Athamantis, in a land of wild animals (wolves).
[63] Finglass 2014:72n53.

Fragment 422

> πολλοὶ παρῆσαν, ἀλλ' ἄπιστα Θεσσαλῶν

Fr. 422 is cited by the scholiast on Aristophanes *Plutus* 521 b Chantry (3.4a.94) as a proverbial phrase about Thessalians' untrustworthiness, especially in slave dealing (διαβάλλονται δὲ οἱ Θετταλοὶ ὡς ἀνδραποδισταὶ καὶ ἄπιστοι). The fragment is paraphrased by Demosthenes 1.21 τὰ τῶν Θετταλῶν ἄπιστα δήπου φύσει ταῦτα καὶ ἀεὶ πᾶσιν ἀνθρώποις (also τοῦτο δὴ πρῶτον αὐτὸν [Φίλιππον] ταράττει ..., εἶτα τὰ τῶν Θετταλῶν. ταῦτα γὰρ ἄπιστα μὲν ἦν δήπου φύσει καὶ ἀεὶ πᾶσιν ἀνθρώποις, κομιδῇ δ', ὥσπερ ἦν, καὶ ἔστι νῦν τούτῳ). Demosthenes' paraphrase as well as Aristophanes' verse line from the *Plutus* are quoted in the Scholia on Euripides *Phoenissae* 1408 Schwartz (1.392.12).

ἄπιστα here means untrustworthy. Cf. Homer *Odyssey* 14.150 κεῖνον ἐλεύσεσθαι, θυμὸς δέ τοι αἰὲν ἄπιστος; Herodotus 1.8.2 ὦτα γὰρ τυγχάνει ἀνθρώποισι ἐόντα ἀπιστότερα ὀφθαλμῶν; Thucydides 8.66.5 καὶ τὸ ἄπιστον οὗτοι μέγιστον πρὸς τοὺς πολλοὺς ἐποίησαν καὶ πλεῖστα ἐς τὴν τῶν ὀλίγων ἀσφάλειαν ὠφέλησαν, βεβαίαν τὴν ἀπιστίαν τῷ δήμῳ πρὸς ἑαυτὸν καταστήσαντες.

Fragment 423

> δ' ἄρα;

Fr. 423 is cited by Hesychius δ 256 Latte δ' ἄρα· ὡς δή. Εὐριπίδης Ἰνοῖ. But, since δ 255 Latte δ' ἄρ'· δή precedes, Kannicht considers it probable that in δ 256 *lemma* δ' ἄρα is hidden, in accordance with the *Iphigenia in Aulis* 1228 (τί δ' ἄρ' ἐγὼ σέ; πρέσβυν ἄρ' ἐκδέξομαι;) and Aristophanes *Peace* 1240 (τί δ' ἄρα τῇ σάλπιγγι τῇδε χρήσομαι;).[64]

For δ' ἄρα (not interrogative), cf. *Bacchae* 164–165 ... ἡδομέ- / να δ' ἄρα πῶλος ὅπως ἅμα ματέρι; see Schmidt 1871:220, who deletes Ἰνοῖ from Hesychius δ 256 Latte (δ' ἄρα· ὡς δή. Εὐριπίδης {Ἰνοῖ}).

---

[64] Kannicht TrGF 5.1 *ad loc.*

1.2.2 The *Oxyrhynchus Papyrus* 5131 (Luppe and Henry)

```
                              ]επτε.[              ]..τ.[
                      ]       χαυνα[
                      _____
                      ]          ἄλλη συνε.[
                      ]          οἵδε γὰρ ἤκουσ[ι...].τ.[.].ολ[
       5      ]υ                 φοράδην τὴν.βαρυδαίμονα[
                                 Κάδμου γενε[......].[
                                 πρὸς+δεσπόσ[υνον δ]ῶμα φέρ[οντες.
                      _____
                      ]    Ἀθάμας  θέσθ' ἡσύχ[......νιν οἱ π[έλας πρὸ.[
                      ]       β    μικρὸν μὲν ὑμῖν ἄχθος, ἀλγειν[ὸν δ' ἐμοί.
       10     ]                   γυμνοῦτε, δείκνυτ' εἰς φάος πο[
                      ]           μὴ καὶ λε....ς ἐν πέπλοισιν[
              ]  ..[              ].ε ψυχα..μοχ.[]    [
                      ].          [.]...[...]ακιβ.[.]ων [
                                 .].. [ ......ἀ]εικέλιος ὤ ταλαπ[ειρι
       15                             ]ων δύστηνος [
                                      ]ελι[|τ]]..α..α....[
                                      ]ανο[..].      [
                                      ]ας         [
                                      ]ο δυστην[
       20                             stripped
                                      ].ν.[
                                      ].ροφαι[
                                      ]..αδεσ[
                                      ]..ωτλαστ[
       25                             ]ησασ[|εκ|].[
                                      ]        [
                                      ]ματω.[
                                      ].ονω.[
```

1–2. The saved text in the first two verse lines is too scanty to lead itself to a conclusion. However, after verse line 2 there is a vestigial paragraph, verified by a horizontal alignment of traces, though with no indication of the name of a speaker. This means that after verse line 2 there is a change not of the speaker, but of the *logos* that is delivered. Since, then, in verses 3–7 the meter is different (anapestic), we may suppose that verses 1–2 are the end of a lyric that is sung by the chorus.

3–7. Recitative dimeter anapests, in which the chorus announce the arrival of a group of male persons (4 οἵδε γὰρ ἥκουσ[ι).

4. ἥκουσ[ι: the present tense of the verb ἥκω has the meaning of perfect tense; so, we are right to suppose that the arrivals have entered the scenic space.

5–7. The members of the group are attendants carrying a person whom they connect with a great and heavy misfortune of Cadmus' family (τὴν βαρυδαίμονα[/ Κάδμου γενε[...).

5–6. The reconstructions suggested here vary with the gender of the person carried by the attendants. P. J. Parsons suggests τὴν βαρυδαίμονα [θήραν] / Κάδμου γενε[ᾶς γέννημα νέον, with the hypothesis that the attendants carry the dead body of Ino's son Learchus whom Athamas has killed while hunting, according to the current myth (as at Sophocles *Philoctetes* 1146 and Euripides *Bacchae* 1144 θήρα δυσπότμῳ).[65] Though they do not exclude Parsons' hypothesis, Luppe and Henry think that the person carried by the attendants is female, more possibly Ino, who is still alive; and they restore τὴν βαρυδαίμονα [νύμφην / Κάδμου γενε[ᾶς or τὴν βαρυδαίμονα Κάδμου γενε[άν (monometer) or an equivalent dimeter,[66] with the idea that the reference to Cadmus' family at verse line 6 "is easier to account for if there is a reference to Ino."[67]

5. φοράδην: The adverb derives from the verb φέρω and is used for someone carried as a load or on a litter (Euripides *Andromache* 1166–1167 καὶ μὴν ὅδ' ἄναξ ἤδη φοράδην / ... πελάζει; Demosthenes 54.20 καὶ ὑγιὴς ἐξελθὼν φοράδην ἦλθον οἴκαδε).

βαρυδαίμονα: Etymologically, βαρυδαίμων is a person with an evil genius (*daimon*), and then a person who suffers troubles.

In verse line 5 there is no possibility of a normal metrical diaeresis between the two anapests. Instead, there is a quasi-caesura between the two halves of the compound adjective βαρυδαίμονα (βαρυ‖δαιμονα).[68] Finglass doubts the "quasi-caesura in compound adjectives" solution to the metrical anomaly (as he considers it) here by arguing that parallels come from Aeschylus (*Prometheus Bound* 172 καί μ' οὔτι μελιγλώσσοις πειθοῦς ἐπαοιδῆσιν and *Prometheus Solutus* TrGF 3 F 192.4 λίμναν παντοτρόφον Αἰθιόπων), but not from Euripides. He believes that φοράδην "is itself misplaced," and some solution would be found if it came at the end of verse line 5; τὴν βαρυδαίμονα then would fall in the first anapestic meter.[69]

---

[65] Luppe and Henry 2012:20.
[66] Luppe and Henry 2012:24.
[67] Luppe and Henry 2012:20.
[68] This solution to the metrical problem here is accepted by Luppe and Henry 2012:23, in accordance with West 1982:95n56.
[69] Finglass 2014:68nn21–22.

6. Κάδμου γενε[: According to Luppe and Henry, this verse line could be treated as monometer if the papyrus trace to the right is casual. But, since "further traces may have been lost to abrasion," Luppe and Henry consider that verse line 6 is "more probably" dimeter.[70]

γενεά: Meaning generation or family, γενεά usually includes more than one person. Therefore, it is hardly acceptable that Κάδμου γενε[ά here refers to Ino alone.

7. δεσπόσυνος is someone (/something) who (/which) belongs to his/her (/its) master. Cf. *Hecuba* 99 (τὰς δεσποσύνους σκηνὰς προλιποῦσ'[α]), 1294–1295 (τῶν δεσποσύνων πειρασόμεναι / μόχθων); *Iphigenia in Tauris* 439 (εἴθ' εὐχαῖσιν δεσποσύνοις); *Phaethon* fr.773.88 (κόσμον δ' ὑμεναίων δεσποσύνων); Aeschylus *Persians* 587 (δεσποσύνοισιν ἀνάγκαις); *Libation Bearers* 942 (ἐπολολύξατ' ὦ δεσποσύνων δόμων). The adjective is not found in Sophocles.[71]

πρὸς δεσπόσ[υνον δ]ῶμα φέρ[οντες: The real destination of the attendants is the palace of Athamas and his wife, the mistress of the female members of the chorus.

The restoration φέρ[οντες, in accordance with οἵδε γὰρ ἤκουσ[ι, creates an acatalectic anapestic dimeter, which is unusual at the end of a passage of non-lyric (recited) anapests. Finglass agrees with Luppe and Henry, that "perhaps something has dropped out after 7: for example, the scribe may have skipped ahead to a second instance of -ντες at verse line-end concluding the system";[72] and he writes the text by adding a verse line 7a, in which the scribe δῶμα φέροντες (‒ υ υ ‒ ‒) would be an acceptable end of the metrical system of these recited anapests.[73] But, since δῶμα φέρ[οντες (‒ υ υ ‒ ‒) is itself an anapestic monometer and it is not impossible for πρὸς δεσπόσ[υνον to have been misplaced, we could treat verse line 7 as monometer, and transmit πρὸς δεσπόσ[υνον to verse line 6, which will then become an acceptable anapestic dimeter. Thus, the text in verses 6–7 could be Κάδμου γενε[ὰν πρὸς δεσπόσ[υνον / δῶμα φέρ[οντες. One might bring the paradigm of *Hippolytus* 252–260, where the anapestic monometer τῆσδ' ὑπεραλγῶ (260) concludes a series of anapestic dimeters by the Nurse (conveying her anxiety about Medea's passionate sentiments).

After verse 7 there is a new paragraph with the speaker indication AΘAMAC in the margin of the papyrus (perhaps as a scenic indication for a reproduction of the play in the Hellenistic period, to which the papyrus belongs). The

---

[70] Luppe and Henry 2012:23, 24.

[71] For quotations, Luppe and Henry 2012:24.

[72] Luppe and Henry 2012:24.

[73] Finglass 2014:68nn23, 69. Kovacs (2016:3) notes that "marking a lacuna after line 7 is not the only way to deal with the problem"; he transposes verse line 6 to stand after verse line 7 (p. 5).

paragraph is accompanied by the letter beta, which must be considered as an indication of Athamas' deuteragonistic role in the play.[74]

8–11. The verses are spoken by Athamas (according to the papyrus indication); and they are iambic trimeters.

8. θέσθ(ε): imperative mood.

ἡσύχ[ως: With composure (*Suppliants* 305 κάρτ' ἂν εἶχον ἡσύχως; *Heracleidae* 7 ἐξὸν κατ' Ἄργος ἡσύχως ναίειν, and Aeschylus *Suppliant Women* 724 ἀλλ' ἡσύχως χρὴ καὶ σεσωφρονισμένως) or gently (*Orestes* 698 εἰ δ' ἡσύχως τις αὐτὸν ἐντείνοντι).

π]έλας not πύλας is the restoration by Luppe and Henry. They believe that the adverb πέλας will be preceded by the article οἱ for the verse line to have a regular caesura; and they restore πρὸ δ[ωμάτων, which "is not likely to have been paired with the vague nearby." They also think that a direct object (to θέσθ') is necessary, and restore the verse line θέσθ' ἡσύχ[ως νιν οἱ π]έλας, with νιν being the direct object "to which the accusative in the following verse line may stand in apposition, as in Euripides *The Trojan Women* 1156–1157."[75] If we now treat the proposed restoration and consider οἱ as an article, we will read οἱ πέλας as a designation of some persons who are nearby, approaching the palace.[76] But, οἱ could also be a dative of the third person personal pronoun, referring to another person who is nearby the palace. In that case, Athamas would point to that person and indicate to the attendants to place their load beside him/her. Cf. Homer *Iliad* 3.408 ἀλλ' αἰεὶ περὶ κεῖνον ὀΐζε, καί ἑ φύλασσε; 9.376 ἅλις δέ οἱ· ἀλλὰ ἕκηλος ἐρρέτω. Grammatically, of course, the accent of the enclitic word οἱ should be transferred to νιν: θέσθ' ἡσύχ[ως νίν οἱ π[έλας πρὸ δ[ωμάτων.

As regards the accusative personal pronoun νιν, it may be considered either as singular (*Orestes* 1665 ὅς νιν φονεῦσαι μητέρ' ἐξηνάγκασα) or plural (*Suppliants* 1139 βεβᾶσιν. <Χο.> αἰθὴρ ἔχει νιν ἤδη). Thus, we understand that what the attendants carry is either one (νιν: singular) or more persons (νιν: plural), and that Athamas demands their care while they are depositing him/her or them.

9. μικρὸν μὲν ὑμῖν ἄχθος: The load is small to you, the bearers. Athamas' expression means that the person (/persons) carried by the attendants is (/are) not an adult (/adults) but a child (/children).

---

[74] Luppe and Henry 2012:19; Finglass 2014:77–79.
[75] Luppe and Henry 2012:24; for the line beginning they compare *Phoenissae* 762 τρέφ' ἀξίως νιν σοῦ τε τήν τ' ἐμὴν χάριν (despite that it belongs to a suspect part of the play).
[76] Finglass 2014:74n62.

μικρὸν, not πικρὸν, is the suggestion by Luppe and Henry.[77] Finglass agrees and rightly observes that πικρὸν, accompanied by ἀλγειν[ὸν δ' ἐμοί, "would wrongly put the focus on the emotional state of the mute attendants rather than of Athamas himself ... it would not be in the manner of tragedy to emphasize their sadness without even mentioning the sorrow of a main character."[78]

ἀλγειν[ὸν δ' ἐμοί: The epithet ἀλγεινόν (painful) creates strong contrast with the light load carried by the attendants. Luppe and Henry consider the restorations ἀλγειν[ὸν δ' ὅμως (in accordance with *Helen* 268 βαρὺ μέν, οἰστέον δ' ὅμως and *Orestes* 230 ἀνιαρὸν ὂν τὸ κτῆμ', ἀναγκαῖον δ' ὅμως) or ἀλγειν[όν θ' ἅμα (in accordance with *Hippolytus* 348 ἥδιστον, ὦ παῖ, ταὐτὸν ἀλγεινόν θ' ἅμα) to be less likely.[79] Athamas' metaphorical characterization of the load as painful shows that the child (/children) carried by the attendants is (/are) his own; and that he is (/they are) at least sick or injured, if not dead.

10-11. γυμνοῦτε ... ἐν πέπλοισιν: Both expressions (γυμνοῦτε and ἐν πέπλοισιν) are used in funeral rites.[80] For γυμνοῦτε Luppe and Henry bring as a parallel *Hecuba* 679 σῶμα γυμνωθὲν νεκροῦ.[81] Πέπλος is usually a female dress (Homer *Iliad* 5.315 πρόσθε δέ οἱ πέπλοιο φαεινοῦ πτύγμα κάλυψεν [for Aphrodite]; *Odyssey* 18.292 Ἀντινόῳ μὲν ἔνεικε μέγαν περικαλλέα πέπλον [for Penelope]; Pindar *Pythian* 9.120 ἀμφί οἱ ψαύσειε πέπλοις [for a Libyan maiden]; Aeschylus *Libation Bearers* 30-31 πρόστερνοι στολμοὶ πέπλων ἀγελάστοις / ξυμφοραῖς πεπληγμένων [the female chorus]). However, in tragedy πέπλος may refer to men's clothing (*Helen* 567 μὴ θίγῃς ἐμῶν πέπλων [Menelaus]; *Bacchae* 938 τἀνθένδε δ' ὀρθῶς παρὰ τένοντ' ἔχει πέπλος [Pentheus]).[82] But the plural πέπλοι, especially in the dative πέπλοις/πέπλοισιν, is used for the wrapping of a dead body, mostly in Euripides' plays: *Heracleidae* 560-561; *Hippolytus* 1457-1458; *Hecuba* 432-434, 577-578, 733-735; *Heracles* 327-335, 701-703; *The Trojan Women* 376-379, 1142-1144, 1218-1220; *Helen* 1241-1243; *Electra* 1227-1232. Cf. Aeschylus *Agamemnon* 1580-1581 ἰδὼν ὑφαντοῖς ἐν πέπλοις Ἐρινύων / τὸν ἄνδρα τόνδε κείμενον; Homer *Iliad* 24.795-796 καὶ τά γε χρυσείην ἐς λάρνακα θῆκαν ἑλόντες / πορφυρέοις πέπλοισι καλύψαντες μαλακοῖσιν.[83]

10. ἐς φάος. Luppe and Henry bring *Hippolytus* 714 ἐς φάος δείξειν as a parallel passage. At the end of verse line 10 they suggest the restoration πό[λει

---

[77] Luppe and Henry 2012:24.
[78] Finglass 2014:66n6. For arguments supporting πικρόν, see Kovacs 2016:5.
[79] Luppe and Henry 2012:24.
[80] See the detailed analysis by Finglass 2014:67-68.
[81] Luppe and Henry 2012:24.
[82] Lee 2012:182-183. I need to note that the plural πέπλοι is also used in the transvestism scene of Pentheus (*Bacchae* 935 ζωναί τε χαλῶσι κοὐχ ἑξῆς πέπλων); but Pentheus' costume in that scene prepares his *sparagmos* by the maenads on Cithaeron.
[83] For the quotations, Finglass 2014:67-68nn16-18.

βλέπειν in accordance with Sophocles *Electra* 1458–1459 κἀναδεικνύναι … ὁρᾶν, *Oedipus Tyrannus* 791–792 … γένος δ᾽ / ἄτλητον ἀνθρώποισι δηλώσοιμ᾽ ὁρᾶν, and Pindar *Nemean* 6.8 τεκμαίρει {δὲ} καί νυν Ἀλκιμίδας τὸ συγγενὲς ἰδεῖν. Their idea is that δείκνυτ᾽ εἰς φάος means uncover, which rather extinguishes the objection that none of the passages they bring as parallel contains εἰς φάος or something comparable. The restoration πο[θῶ βλέπειν (preceded by punctuation) is considered to be only "a theoretical possibility," since it makes "little contribution to the sense."[84]

11. μὴ καὶ λεληθώς: The restoration is suggested as "suitable to the theme of a shrouded body." Moreover, Luppe and Henry think that "it would confirm that the body is that of a male."[85] If this hypothesis is valid and the participle λεληθώς refers to the dead, we must accept that what the attendants carry is one corpse, that of Athamas' older son, Learchus, whom Athamas himself killed in the hunting. But it is not necessarily right that the participle λεληθώς refers only to the dead. It may very well have Athamas as its subject who in devastation asks (in first person singular) for the funeral pall to be pulled. This is the meaning of the verb λέληθα when it is used with an infinitive, and the syntactical link of the verb λέληθα with an infinitive cannot be excluded from this particular passage. Cf. Pindar *Pythian* 5.23 … τῶ σε μὴ λαθέτω, / Κυράνᾳ γλυκὺν ἀμφὶ κᾶ- / πον Ἀφροδίτας ἀειδόμενον, / παντὶ μὲν θεὸν αἴτιον ὑπερτιθέμεν, / φιλεῖν δὲ Κάρρωτον ἔξοχ᾽ ἑταίρων (… Therefore, do not forget, as you are being sung of at the sweet garden of Aphrodite in Kyrene, to give credit to the god for everything, but to cherish above all comrades Karrhotos. Translation by Race 1997).

At the end of verse line 11 the restoration proposed is πέπλοις or πέπλοισι(ν), followed by a verb in the subjunctive mood (e.g. εὑρεθῇ, ἐγκρυφῇ, εἰσίη). Luppe and Henry translate "enter" the palace and mention the πρόθεσις as the aim of the arrival of the attendants.[86]

After verse line 11 there is a new paragraph with some traces barely preserved; they point to the name of a speaker accompanied by an alpha. Luppe and Henry restore only the name of Ino, and this very cautiously;[87] however, Finglass thinks that the restoration is valid and should be considered of Ino as protagonist.[88]

12–28. If Ino is the speaker, she laments for the child murdering.

---

[84] Luppe and Henry 2012:24.
[85] Luppe and Henry 2012:24. Kovacs (2016:5) adds <ἐμπνέῃ> after πέπλοισιν with the idea that Athamas hopes his son is still alive.
[86] The scene is relevant to that of the customary πρόθεσις of the dead; see Garland 2001:23–30. Euripides' tragedies (especially *Alcestis*, *Suppliants*, and *The Trojan Women*) provide pictures of customary funeral rites; see Mikalson 1991:121–128.
[87] Luppe and Henry 2012:25.
[88] Finglass 2014:66.

12.].ε ψυχα . . μοχ . [ ]

Luppe and Henry think that ψυχασεμοχθ, however it may be articulated, is a possible restoration, though it cannot be confirmed; they also consider ψυχαδ (ψυχὰ δ', δὲ) as a possibility, but with great cautiousness about the traces of the letter δ.

μοχθηρός: either a person who suffers misfortunes (Aeschylus *Seven Against Thebes* 257 μοχθηρόν [γυναικῶν γένος]—ὥσπερ ἄνδρας ὧν ἁλῷ πόλις; Sophocles *Philoctetes* 254 ὦ πόλλ' ἐγὼ μοχθηρός) or a person who causes misfortunes (Herodotus 7.46.4 οὕτω ὁ μὲν θάνατος μοχθηρῆς ἐούσης τῆς ζόης καταφυγὴ αἱρετωτάτη τῷ ἀνθρώπῳ γέγονε, ὁ δὲ θεὸς γλυκὺν γεύσας τὸν αἰῶνα φθονερὸς ἐν αὐτῷ εὑρίσκεται ἐών; Sophocles *Electra* 599–600 ἢ ζῶ βίον μοχθηρόν, / ἔκ τε σοῦ κακοῖς / πολλοῖς ἀεὶ ξυνοῦσα; Aristophanes *Thesmophoriazusae* 781 τουτὶ τὸ ῥῶ μοχθηρόν).

ψυχά: the Ionic form of the singular nominative/vocative ψυχή (*psyche*) or the Attic form of the dual nominative (/accusative/vocative) ψυχά (for two persons); the latter is reinforced by the ending ε (*e*) of the previous (lost) word, which might be the dual demonstrative pronoun τώδε, referring to the souls of Athamas' two murdered children (τώδε ψυχά). Ino rather refers to her soul as suffering misfortunes[89] or to the soul of her unfortunate (killed) child (/two children). If the carried corpses are two and it is Ino who laments for their death, the papyric text may be the unique one that justifies what the chorus says in the *Medea* (1282–1289) about Ino's crime against her own children in a state of mania. In that case it raises great doubt about the credibility of the ending verse lines of Hyginus' *Fabula* 4, referring to the common mythic narrative about Hera's wrath against Ino and Athamas.

13. [καμ]ακι βα[λ]ών is the restoration proposed by Luppe and Henry, with the idea that the text refers to the killing of Learchus, though in Apollodorus 1.9.2 the fatal weapon is not a spear-shaft but an arrow; in their proposal, βαλών could be the end of a dochmiac meter.

14. ἀ]εικέλιος ὦ ταλαπ[ειρι is the restoration by Luppe and Henry; μόρος ἀ]εικέλιος is the proposal by Parsons.

ἀεικέλιος means cruel/brutal/foul for things or words. See Homer *Odyssey* 4.244 αὐτόν μιν πληγῇσιν ἀεικελίῃσι δαμάσσας (marring his own body with cruel blows) and 19.341 πολλὰς γὰρ δὴ νύκτας ἀεικελίῳ ἐνὶ κοίτῃ / ἄεσα καί τ' ἀνέμεινα ἐΰθρονον Ἠῶ δῖαν (for many a night have I lain upon a foul bed and waited for the bright-throned Dawn. Translation by Murray 1919). It also means uncouth or timorous for persons (Homer *Iliad* 14.84–85 οὐλόμεν' αἴθ' ὤφελλες ἀεικελίου

---

[89] Finglass 2014:75n70 thinks that ψυχά here is an invocation of Ino's own soul at the start point of her threnos.

στρατοῦ ἄλλου / σημαίνειν [doomed man that thou art, would that thou wert in command of some other, inglorious army]; *Odyssey* 6.242–243 πρόσθεν μὲν γὰρ δή μοι ἀεικέλιος δέατ' εἶναι, / νῦν δὲ θεοῖσιν ἔοικε, τοὶ οὐρανὸν εὐρὺν ἔχουσιν [before he seemed to me uncouth, but now he is like the gods, who hold broad heaven] for the feminine gender in particular). Cf. the adverb ἀεικελίως in Homer *Odyssey* 8.231–232 (λίην γὰρ ἀεικελίως ἐδαμάσθην / κύμασιν ἐν πολλοῖς [for cruelly have I been broken amid the many waves]) and Bacchylides 3.45–46 (ἀεικελίως γυναῖκες / ἐξ ἐϋκτίτων μεγάρων ἄγονται [the women are shamefully carried off of the well-built halls] Translation by Campbell 1992). See also αἰκέλιος in the *Andromache* 131 (δέμας αἰκέλιον καταλείβειν [to mar your body with weeping in bewilderment] Translation by Kovacs 1995) and Theognis 1344 (οὐ γὰρ ἐπ' αἰκελίῳ παιδὶ δαμεὶς ἐφάνην [for this no unhandsome lad I am seen to be taken with] Translation by Edmonds 1931).[90]

ταλαπείριος may be used for ταλαίπωρος in tragedy according to the Etymologicum Genuinum and Photius. Luppe and Henry propose ὦ ταλαπ[είριε or ὦ ταλαπείριος; or ω may represent ᾧ. The synonymous epithet ταλαπενθής, which begins with the same letters, would be a possible restoration, but it is attested only in epic (Homer *Odyssey* 5.222 τλήσομαι ἐν στήθεσσιν ἔχων ταλαπενθέα θυμόν) and Bacchylides (5.157–158 τέγξαι βλέφαρον, ταλαπενθέος / πότμον οἰκτίροντα φωτός and 16.26 πύθετ' ἀγγελίαν ταλαπενθέα). From ancient citations mentioning ταλαίπωρος or ταλαιπωρῶ, it appears that the meaning of this wording usually denotes the element of duration in the sufferings of an unhappy person. See *Electra* 334 αἱ χεῖρες ἡ γλῶσσ' ἡ ταλαίπωρός τε φρήν; *Orestes* 672 ταλαιπωρεῖν με δεῖ; Aeschylus *Prometheus Bound* 231 βροτῶν δὲ τῶν ταλαιπώρων λόγον; Sophocles *Oedipus at Colonus* 14 πάτερ ταλαίπωρ' Οἰδίπους; Thucydides 2.101.5 καὶ ἡ στρατιὰ σῖτόν τε οὐκ εἶχεν αὐτῷ καὶ ὑπὸ χειμῶνος ἐταλαιπώρει; Lysias 31.12 οὔτε γὰρ τῷ σώματι ἀδύνατος ἦν ταλαιπωρεῖν; Demosthenes 2.16 λυποῦνται καὶ συνεχῶς ταλαιπωροῦσιν. Thus, in our scanty text, ταλαπείριος, following ἀ]εικέλιος, is more likely to characterize not the short life of a dead infant, but the lamenting Ino, in a manner of self-referentiality denoting her sufferings, which now culminate in the murder of her child/children. Luppe and Henry think that ἀ]εικέλιος ὦ ταλαπ[ειρι˘ may be the end of one dochmiac and the whole of the next.

15.]ων δύστηνος [: Luppe and Henry consider the meter to be dochmiac[91] and suggest word-end before ˘]ων δύστηνος and a participle, e.g. θαν]ών, as the first word of the dochmiac. However, one could think of a noun (e.g. κακῶν) instead of a participle; cf. Aeschylus *Persians* 909 δύστηνος ἐγώ, στυγερᾶς μοίρας

---

[90] Luppe and Henry (*ad loc.*) mention that αἰκέλιος is seldom used of persons and is not found elsewhere in tragedy.

[91] According to West 1982:110.

37

(for the lamenting Xerxes), where the epithet δύστηνος is followed by the genitive στυγερᾶς μοίρας (an object to κυρήσας, 910) for Xerxes' cruel doom. In our text, δύστηνος, considered to be connected syntactically with the genitive κακῶν, would refer to the lamenting Ino, who, like Xerxes, cries for her miserable fate. Covacs (2016:6) considers δύστηνος (with Attic η) to be incompatible with lyric and suggests an alternation between threnetic passages by Ino and spoken passages by Athamas. In Aeschylus' *Persians* δύστηνος belongs to an anapestic passage, as Xerxes enters the theatrical stage. So, we could also think of placing the epithet δύστηνος in an *epirrhematic* exchange that includes lyrics sung by Ino and anapests uttered by Athamas.

16. Luppe and Henry correct λιτον to λιθον.

17. The restoration ἀνο[σί]ῳ is proposed by Luppe and Henry very cautiously (with a question mark).

22.]τροφαι or στροφαι are both suggested as probable.

24. Luppe and Henry read ωτλας and search for a possible restoration in *Alcestis* 837 ὦ πολλὰ τλᾶσα καρδία καὶ χεὶρ ἐμή and *Ion* 1497 ὦ δεινὰ τλᾶσα, μῆτερ. From the traces of the papyrus they are driven to suggest a divider after the first letter-trace and a ὑφ' ἕν under ω. Their idea is that "the corrector may have intended to show that ωτλα- forms a unit (ὦ + ατλα- in cras?)" and that "perhaps two lines had mistakenly been run together (as in Bachylides 13.159–160) and the corrector simply wished to indicate the correct division." But no further supposition can be made for the continuation. However scanty it may be, the wording in verses 12–25 (ταλαπείριος ἀεικέλιος, δύστηνος, τλᾶσα) rather safely suggests a threnetic passage after filicide with Ino as the most probable speaker.

Two general observations on the papyric passage: (a) The fact that surely Athamas and probably Ino are involved in this scene in a condition of great grief suggests that they both participate in the πρόθεσις of their killed child/children not in a state of mania, but in a state of sanity. (b) The sequence between the sung and recited verse lines of the passage suggests a dramatic synthesis that is rather unique, as Athamas' four iambic trimeters intervene between the chorus' recited and Ino's lyric threnos. Finglass searches for a parallel in Euripides' *The Trojan Women* (235–238), where Talthybius' four iambic trimeters, which are followed by Hecuba's threnetic response, are preceded by five anapestic dimeters by the chorus (230–234), concluding a lyric interchange between them and (the protagonist) Hecuba (98–229).[92] There is, however, a notable difference. In *The Trojan Women* Talthybius acts simply as a messenger who brings the bad news to Hecuba; in our passage Athamas is emotionally involved in the dramatic events.

---

[92] Finglass 2014:68.

2

Reconstruction Matters

2.1 Mythographical Sources

Before my reconstruction attempt, what I need to discuss is the work of the later mythographers who collected all different—sometimes contradictory—versions of the story of Ino, Athamas, and the Athamantidae, and tried to arrange them in their narratives.

2.1.1 Apollodorus *Library*

The first mythographic narration about Ino, Athamas, and the Athamantidae is found in the first book of Apollodorus' *Library* (1.9.1–2). According to this narrative, Athamas was a king of Thessaly. His first wife was Nephele, who bore him Phrixus and Helle. Ino was his second wife and bore him two sons, Learchus and Melicertes. Because of her jealousy, Ino plotted evil against Nephele's children. She convinced the women of the country to roast wheat spores, without their men knowing, which then of course did not yield a crop, and then convinced Athamas' messengers to go to Delphi in order to dispel the forces of evil onto Nephele's children, and to relay a command to the Delphic king to sacrifice Phrixus to Zeus. But Nephele was able to avert the slaughter by snatching her children and placing them on Hermes' ram with the golden fleece who took Phrixus and Helle to the Black Sea. After some more details about Helle's drowning and Phrixus' reception by Aeetes in his land (Colchis), Apollodorus completes his narrative with Athamas' punishment by the enraged Hera without any reference to the cause of the goddess' ira (1.9.2). In a state of mania, Athamas kills his older son Learchus, while Ino falls with her younger son Melicertes into the sea; exiled then, Athamas leaves Boiotia and, according to an oracle, builds his own country, the Athamantis, in a land of wild animals (wolves), where he married Themisto, who bore him four sons, Leucon, Erythius, Schoeneus, and Ptous:

τῶν δὲ Αἰόλου παίδων Ἀθάμας, Βοιωτίας δυναστεύων, ἐκ Νεφέλης τεκνοῖ παῖδα μὲν Φρίξον θυγατέρα δὲ Ἕλλην. αὖθις δὲ Ἰνὼ γαμεῖ, ἐξ ἧς αὐτῷ Λέαρχος καὶ Μελικέρτης ἐγένοντο. ἐπιβουλεύουσα δὲ Ἰνὼ τοῖς Νεφέλης τέκνοις ἔπεισε τὰς γυναῖκας τὸν πυρὸν φρύγειν. λαμβάνουσαι δὲ κρύφα τῶν ἀνδρῶν τοῦτο ἔπρασσον. γῆ δὲ πεφρυγμένους πυροὺς δεχομένη καρποὺς ἐτησίους οὐκ ἀνεδίδου. διὸ πέμπων ὁ Ἀθάμας εἰς Δελφοὺς ἀπαλλαγὴν ἐπυνθάνετο τῆς ἀφορίας. Ἰνὼ δὲ τοὺς πεμφθέντας ἀνέπεισε λέγειν ὡς εἴη κεχρησμένον παύσεσθαι τὴν ἀκαρπίαν, ἐὰν σφαγῇ Διὶ ὁ Φρίξος. τοῦτο ἀκούσας Ἀθάμας, συναναγκαζόμενος ὑπὸ τῶν τὴν γῆν κατοικούντων, τῷ βωμῷ παρέστησε Φρίξον. Νεφέλη δὲ μετὰ τῆς θυγατρὸς αὐτὸν ἀνήρπασε, καὶ παρ' Ἑρμοῦ λαβοῦσα χρυσόμαλλον κριὸν ἔδωκεν, ὑφ' οὗ φερόμενοι δι' οὐρανοῦ γῆν ὑπερέβησαν καὶ θάλασσαν ... Ἀθάμας δὲ ὕστερον διὰ μῆνιν Ἥρας καὶ τῶν ἐξ Ἰνοῦς ἐστερήθη παίδων· αὐτὸς μὲν γὰρ μανεὶς ἐτόξευσε Λέαρχον, Ἰνὼ δὲ Μελικέρτην μεθ' ἑαυτῆς εἰς πέλαγος ἔρριψεν. ἐκπεσὼν δὲ τῆς Βοιωτίας ἐπυνθάνετο τοῦ θεοῦ ποῦ κατοικήσει· χρησθέντος δὲ αὐτῷ κατοικεῖν ἐν ᾧπερ ἂν τόπῳ ὑπὸ ζῴων ἀγρίων ξενισθῇ, πολλὴν χώραν διελθὼν ἐνέτυχε λύκοις προβάτων μοίρας νεμομένοις· οἱ δέ, θεωρήσαντες αὐτόν, ἃ διηροῦντο ἀπολιπόντες ἔφυγον. Ἀθάμας δὲ κτίσας τὴν χώραν Ἀθαμαντίαν ἀφ' ἑαυτοῦ προσηγόρευσε, καὶ γήμας Θεμιστὼ τὴν Ὑψέως ἐγέννησε Λεύκωνα Ἐρύθριον Σχοινέα Πτῶον.[1]

Apollodorus Library 1.9.1–2

Athamas, one of the sons of Aiolos, ruled Boiotia and fathered by Nephele a son, Phrixos, and a daughter, Helle. He married a second wife, Ino, and had by her Learchos and Melicertes. Ino plotted against the children of Nephele and persuaded the women to parch the wheat. The women got hold of it without their husbands' knowing and did just that. The earth, because it was planted with parched wheat, did not yield its annual crop. Because of this Athamas sent to Delphi to ask how to end the famine. Ino convinced the men he sent to tell him that it had been prophesied that the crop failure would end if Phrixos were sacrificed to Zeus. When Athamas heard this, he brought Phrixos to the altar, but only after being forced by the inhabitants of his country to do so. Nephele, however, snatched Phrixos up along with her daughter and

---

[1] The text from Frazer 1921.

gave them a ram with golden fleece that she had gotten from Hermes. Riding it through the sky, they traversed land and sea. When they were over the sea lying between Sigeion and the Chersonesos, Helle slipped off and fell into the deep. Because she died there, the sea is called the Hellespont after her ... Because of Hera's wrath Athamas later also lost the children born to him by Ino. He was driven mad and shot Learchos with an arrow, and Ino threw herself and Melicertes into the sea. Driven out of Boiotia, Athamas asked the god where he should make his home. The oracle's response told him to settle in whatever place he was treated as a guest by wild animals. After passing through a lot of territory, he met with some wolves feeding on portions of sheep. But when they caught sight of him, they abandoned the food they were sharing and fled. Athamas settled the area and called the country Athamantia after himself. He married Themisto, daughter of Hypseus, and fathered Leucon, Erythrios, Schoineus, and Ptoos.[2]

Hera's *ira* against Athamas and Ino also exists in Apollodorus' third book, where all the mythological facts surrounding Ino's relationship to Dionysus are found to be systematized in a general frame of reference to the birth of Dionysus. The *Library* here refers to Ino as the wife of Athamas and explains Hera's jealous revenge. The goddess seems to have induced madness in Ino and Athamas because they received and nursed little Dionysus after his birth from the thigh of Zeus after Semele had been struck by lightning:

ἀποθανούσης δὲ Σεμέλης, αἱ λοιπαὶ Κάδμου θυγατέρες διήνεγκαν λόγον, συνηυνῆσθαι θνητῷ τινι Σεμέλην καὶ καταψεύσασθαι Διός, καὶ ὅτι διὰ τοῦτο ἐκεραυνώθη. κατὰ δὲ τὸν χρόνον τὸν καθήκοντα Διόνυσον γεννᾷ Ζεὺς λύσας τὰ ῥάμματα, καὶ δίδωσιν Ἑρμῇ. ὁ δὲ κομίζει πρὸς Ἰνὼ καὶ Ἀθάμαντα καὶ πείθει τρέφειν ὡς κόρην. ἀγανακτήσασα δὲ Ἥρα μανίαν αὐτοῖς ἐνέβαλε, καὶ Ἀθάμας μὲν τὸν πρεσβύτερον παῖδα Λέαρχον ὡς ἔλαφον θηρεύσας ἀπέκτεινεν, Ἰνὼ δὲ τὸν Μελικέρτην εἰς πεπυρωμένον λέβητα ῥίψασα, εἶτα βαστάσασα μετὰ νεκροῦ τοῦ παιδὸς ἥλατο κατὰ βυθοῦ. καὶ Λευκοθέα μὲν αὐτὴ καλεῖται, Παλαίμων δὲ ὁ παῖς.

Apollodorus Library 3.4.3

After Semele's death, the remaining daughters of Cadmos spread a story that Semele had been sleeping with some mortal man and had faked her affair with Zeus, and that that was why she was struck by a thunderbolt. When the proper time came, Zeus gave birth to Dionysos

---

[2] The translation by S. M. Trzaskoma, in Smith and Trzaskoma 2007.

by undoing his stitches. He gave him to Hermes, who brought him to Ino and Athamas and convinced them to raise him as a girl. Hera was enraged and cast madness upon them. Athamas hunted down and killed their oldest son, Learchos, thinking that he was a deer. Ino threw Melicertes into a boiling cauldron, then took him and jumped into the deep with her son's corpse. She is called Leucothea, and her son is called Palaemon, having been given these names by sailors, for the two of them help those caught in storms.

Prima facie, Apollodorus' second narrative adds elements that simply explain Heras' ira. But carefully considered, Hera's wrath here is given as a separate event, independent of Ino's plotting against Nephele's children. The detail that Ino boiled her son before she leapt with him into the deep sea, which is omitted from the narrative about Ino's plotting against Nephele's children in the first book, confirms Ino's mania inspired in her by Hera. Without it, Ino's fall with Melicertes into the sea is not necessary to be associated with mania; it could easily be considered as an instantaneous reaction by Ino to Athamas' mania. One may thus understand that the writer of the *Library* did not need to express the elements of Ino's mania against Melicertes in the framework of his narrative about Ino's plotting against Nephele's children in the first book; he simply completed his story by adding the well-known punishment of the couple Ino and Athamas because of Hera's wrath. In his narrative, however, about Dionysus' birth in the third book, where Ino's affinity to Dionysus is prior to her actions as a jealous wife, Hera's wrath against Ino as a nurse of Dionysus is rightly accorded appropriate space so that the mania inspired in Ino by the goddess is completely presented.

2.1.2 Hyginus *Fabulae*

The Latin mythographer Hyginus (first century CE) organizes his work in a different manner: he writes separate stories (named *Fabulae*) among which he includes special narratives referring to particular dramas. This is an indication that some of the later mythographers (Hyginus at least) took into account myths composed by tragic poets, particularly if they were different from what was mythologically current. This is exactly the case of Hyginus' *Fabula* 4 about Euripides' *Ino* and *Fabula* 8 about Ennius' *Antiope*. For the mythical account of Ino, Athamas, and the Athamantidae, Hyginus devotes four narratives: *Fabula* 1 entitled *Themisto*, *Fabula* 2 entitled *Ino*, *Fabula* 3 entitled *Phrixus*, and *Fabula* 5 entitled *Athamas*. From them, *Fabula* 3 refers to Phrixus' adventures in Colchis, in which my study is not interested; and the very short *Fabula* 5 is restricted only to Athamas' fate, that he killed his son while hunting in a state of mania inspired by the jealous Hera.

The story of *Fabula* 1 about Themisto does not exist in Apollodorus. Themisto here is referred to as the second wife of Athamas, after Nephele and before Ino. The crucial theme of the narrative is Themisto's jealousy against Ino. Themisto plots the killing of Ino's children, but an anonymous nurse dresses Themisto's children as the targeted victims because she pities Ino. Themisto thus unwillingly kills her own children and then commits suicide when she realizes the truth:

> Athamas Aeoli filius habuit ex Nebula uxore filium Phrixum et filiam Hellen, et ex Themisto Hypsei filia filios duos, Sphincium et Orchomenum, et ex Ino Cadmi filia filios duos, Learchum et Melicerten. Themisto, quod se Ino congugio privasset, filios ejus interficere voluit; itaque in regia latuit clam et occasione nacta, cum putaret se inimicae natos interfecisse, suos imprudens occidit, a nutrice decepta quod eis vestem perperam injecerat. Themisto cognita re ipsa se interfecit.[3]

Hyginus *Fabula* 1

> Athamas son of Aeolus had by his wife, Nebula, a son, Phrixus, and a daughter, Helle. By Themisto daughter of Hypseus he had two sons, Sphincius and Orchomenus. And by Ino daughter of Cadmus he had two sons, Learchus and Melicertes. Themisto wanted to kill Ino's sons because Ino had ruined her marriage. And so she hid secretly in the palace, and when the occasion presented itself, she killed her own children without realizing it. She thought that she was killing those of her rival, but she was misled by the fact that the children's nurse had dressed them in the wrong clothing. When Themisto realized what she had done, she committed suicide.[4]

Fabula 2 is similar to Apollodorus' narrative in his first book about Ino's plotting against Nephele's children, but with interesting variations: (a) Phrixus voluntarily proposes to be sacrificed; (b) a priest, who pities Phrixus, reveals Ino's plot to Athamas; (c) Athamas gives Ino and Melicertes to Phrixus to be sacrificed; (d) at the end Dionysus intervenes and saves his nurse Ino:

> Ino Cadmi et Harmoniae filia, cum Phrixum et Hellen ex Nebula natos interficere voluisset, init consilium cum totius generis matronis

---

[3]   The text by Marshall 2002.
[4]   The translation by R. S. Smith, in Smith and Trzaskoma 2007.

et conjuravit ut fruges in sementem quas darent torrerent, ne nascerentur; ita ut, cum sterilitas et penuria frugum esset, civitas tota partim fame, partim morbo interiret. de ea re Delphos mittit Athamas satellitem, cui Ino praecepit ut falsum responsum ita referret: si Phrixum immolasset Iovi, pestilentiae fore finem. quod cum Athamas se facturum abnuisset, Phrixus ultro ac libens pollicetur se unum civitatem aerumna liberaturum. itaque cum ad aram cum infulis esset adductus et pater Iovem comprecari vellet, satelles misericordia adulescentis Inus Athamanti consilium patefecit; rex facinore cognito, uxorem suam Ino et filium ejus Melicerten Phrixo dedit necandos. quos cum ad supplicium duceret, Liber pater ei caliginem iniecit et Ino suam nutricem eripuit. Athamas postea, ab Iunone insania obiecta, Learchum filium interfecit. at Ino cum Melicerte filio suo in mare se praecipitavit; quam Liber Leucotheam voluit appellari, nos Matrem Matutam dicimus, Melicerten autem deum Palaemonem, quem nos Portunum dicimus. huic quinto quoque anno ludi gymnici fiunt, qui appellantur Ἴσθμια.

Hyginus *Fabula* 2

Ino, the daughter of Cadmus and Harmonia, wanted to kill Phrixus and Helle, Athamas' children by Nebula. So she formed a plan involving the women of the entire country and made them all swear that they would parch the grain they were going to supply for sowing, so that it would not sprout. Thus it happened that because of the crop failure and the shortage of grain, the entire population was dying off, some because of starvation, some because of disease. Athamas sent one of his aides to Delphi to inquire about the matter, but Ino ordered him to report a false oracle: if Athamas were to sacrifice Phrixus to Jupiter, there would be an end to the blight. When Athamas refused to do this, Phrixus willingly came forward of his own accord and declared that he would free the state from its plight. When he had been led to the altar dressed in the sacrificial headdress and his father was about to invoke Jupiter, out of pity for the boy Athamas' aide revealed Ino's scheme to Athamas. When the king learned of the crime, he handed his wife, Ino, and her son, Melicertes, over to Phrixus for execution. As Phrixus led them to their punishment, Father Liber enveloped him in a mist and rescued Ino because she had raised him. Later, Athamas was driven mad by Juno and killed his son Learchus. As for Ino, she threw herself and her son Melicertes into the sea. Liber ordained that she be called Leucothea (we call her Mater Matuta) and that Melicertes be called the god Palaemon (we call him Portunus). In his honor every four years athletic games are held, which are called Isthmian.

It is obvious that the last part of the narrative, referring to Hera's ira against Athamas and Ino, is exactly the same as the relevant narrative in Apollodorus' first book; and as well as in Apollodorus, it does not fit well with the narrative itself, looking like a separate addition by the mythographer.

Recounting now Hyginus' *Fabula* 4, referring to Euripides' *Ino*,[5] we first notice that the story (*mythos*) of the play narrated in this fabula by Hyginus is different from the general mythical account narrated about Ino in his *Fabula* 2. And it is relevant to the mythical account of Themisto narrated in his *Fabula* 1, where the core event, Themisto's unconscious filicide, is somewhat similar to that of his *Fabula* 4. There are however differences that are worth noting, since the narrative of *Fabula* 4 mainly consists of the return of Ino-maenad to the house of Athamas, her secret cohabitation with Themisto as a servant, and her plotting against Themisto's children; and it is Ino herself who consciously dresses Themisto's children as the targeted victims in order to save her own sons from Themisto's jealously. Moreover, the narrative of *Fabula* 4 ends similarly to that of *Fabula* 2, with a brief reference to Hera's revenge against Athamas and Ino, but not similarly to the *Fabula* 1, where no reference to Hera's revenge exists. According to Apollodorus *Library* 3.4.3, Hera's revenge of Athamas and Ino by means of mania was primarily connected with the nursing of Dionysus by Ino; so, it was rather alien to jealousy-motivated filicides by Athamas' wives. Thus, it is worth noticing that Hera's mythical account is narrated at the end of the *Fabula* 2 only after the reference to the intervention of Dionysus who saves his nurse, Ino, but it is not included in the narrative of his *Fabula* 1, narrating the plotting of the jealous Themisto against the children of her rival Ino. The fact, therefore, that the mythical account of Hera's ira does exist at the end of *Fabula* 4 is an element that raises the question of whether it really existed in Euripides' *Ino* or was supplied as a valid mythological account about Ino, which Hyginus preferred not to omit.[6]

2.2 Survey of Reconstruction Attempts

My survey of the philological approaches to Euripides' *Ino* will start with the reconstruction of the play by F. G. Welcker[7] and include the proposals offered by

---

[5] For the text see in the Commentary (Chapter 1) p. 3.
[6] See also my cautiousness in the Commentary, *ad loc.* (Chapter 1).
[7] Welcker 1839–1841:2.615–624.

J. A. Hartung,[8] T. Zielinski,[9] T. B. L. Webster,[10] and F. Jouan and H. van Looy.[11] All five proposals will be considered with a critical synthesis of their arguments. The most recent articles by P. Finglass,[12] which are based on the *Oxyrhynchus Papyrus* 5131 and both together try to resolve key problems of the play in the light of the new evidence shed by the papyric fragment, should be discussed separately.

In all reconstruction attempts one thing is common: difficulty in arranging the extant (book) fragments of the *Ino* in an accurate way. Few of these fragments are self-explanatory. Most of them are gnomological, speaking about polygamy and monogamy, the dignity of noble birth, resignation and hope, ideas about which Ino or Athamas or Themisto could argue. Moreover, until the recent publication of the *Oxyrhynchus Papyrus* 5131, Hyginus' *Fabula* 4 was necessarily a source unique to every reconstruction attempt, so that the elements reported by Hyginus were acceptable by scholars even in the cases where they caused their reluctance.

In most of the proposals, the plot of the *Ino* is supposed to consist of a prologue (monologue in its first part at least), a parodos, three or four episodes (each followed by a stasimon), and a *deus ex machina* scene at the end of the play. The dramatic persons are at least Athamas, Ino, and Themisto; and the chorus is surely a female group. Most of the episodes are supposed to be dialogues (sometimes agonistic) between the dramatic persons (between Athamas and Ino, Athamas and Themisto, Ino and Themisto) or/and between a dramatic person and the chorus (Welcker and Hartung propose a dialogic scene between Ino and the chorus; Jouan and van Looy think of a dialogue between Athamas and the chorus). Messenger speeches are suggested to be monologues, one narrating Themisto's crimes and one narrating the killing of Learchus by Athamas while hunting. So, if we attempt to give a representative example of reconstruction of the text of Euripides' *Ino*, the plot would be approximately as follows: prologue (by Athamas or Ino); parodos (by the chorus); first episode (a confrontation between Athamas and Themisto); first stasimon (by the chorus); second episode (Ino's and Themisto's conspiring); second stasimon (by the chorus); third episode (murder of Themisto's children with Ino's plotting); third stasimon (by the chorus); Exodus (a *deus ex machina* narrating Athamas' and Ino's mania, Athamas' murder of Learchus and Ino's fall into the sea with Melicertes); the chorus' exodus.

---

[8] Hartung 1843:1.453–464.
[9] Zielinski 1929.
[10] Webster 1967:98–105.
[11] Jouan and van Looy 2002:190–210.
[12] Finglass 2014 and 2016.

In particular, what is usually suggested for the prologue is related to the Euripidean technique of the monologic prologues, known from his surviving tragedies. Thus, scholars suppose that the prologue of the *Ino* would be a monologue delivered either by Ino or Athamas, who refers to the backbone of the drama. However, their suggestions are differentiated according to the identity of the person proposed as a speaker. For example, when the prologue is attributed to Ino (Welcker, Zielinski), there is a tendency (Zielinski) to include in it references to the heroine's previous crimes (her plotting against Phrixus and Helle), which are narrated in Apollodorus and Hyginus' *Fabula* 2 (*Ino*) but are not found in Hyginus *Fabula* 4 narrating the plot of Euripides' *Ino*. Moreover, there is the idea that in the play Ino repents for her actions (Jouan and van Looy), though in Hyginus' *Fabula* 4 there is no room for such a hypothesis. As regards the dialogic scenes, which, in the proposals of some scholars (Welcker, Webster, Jouan and van Looy), are not few, what is suggested is either an aggressive attitude of Ino against the polygamy of Athamas (Welcker, Hartung, Webster) or, on the contrary, an emphasis on her misfortune, which could be stated through her rags or/and her repentance (Zielinski, Jouan and van Looy).

The detail in *Fabula* 4, that Ino's identity remained unknown to Themisto, is crucial to what scholars suggest about the relationship between the two women. Welcker places the agreement between Themisto and Ino after a series of dialogic scenes between them and Athamas; more specifically, between Athamas and Ino, Athamas and Themisto, and (again) Athamas and Ino. Zielinski stresses Themisto's concern for the return of Ino, whom he represents as unhappy (in rags) but courageous and brave, especially in an *agon* with Athamas, where Ino herself announces the death of Themisto's children. Webster attributes a strong character to both Ino and Themisto, which emerges through a central agonistic scene of the play. He thinks that Ino's silence is not a choice of her own, but a demand given to her. He also argues that there is no exchange of garments covering Themisto's and Ino's children and shows Ino repenting only after the death of Themisto's children. The reconstruction by Jouan and van Looy deviates from Hyginus' *Fabula* 4 in that the chorus recognizes Ino and that it is her humility that persuades Themisto to trust her honesty, and that Ino herself announces in tears her intention to change children's robes.

For the announcement of Themisto's crimes, scholars accept the solution of a messenger speech. However, they do not agree on the identity of the speaker. The most conventional solution has been given by Welcker, who attributes the announcement to an anonymous messenger (*Angelos*). In Hartung's proposal it is Ino herself who announces the horrible murder in front of her own children (Learchus and Melicertes); she then sends the older Learchus to accompany his father hunting and keeps the younger Melicertes with her. With such a suggestion, Hartung opts for understanding the stage representation of Hera's wrath in the *Ino* as a revenge for Ino's involvement in the death of Themisto's children, which is different from the basic idea of the mythical account itself that wanted Hera to punish Ino as a nurse of Dionysus. Zielinski, too, makes Ino a messenger of Themisto's crimes, and represents her proudly announcing the events in an *agon* with Athamas. In his proposal, Hera's punishment does also immediately follow: after his *agon* with Ino, Athamas leaves for hunting and Ino suffers regret for her actions. According to Webster, who disbelieves the exchange of the children's garments, the announcement of the events is attributed to Athamas, who makes Ino regret and implore him to show mercy. In Jouan's and van Looy's proposal, it is a nurse or a paedagogus who announces the events to Athamas. The announcement follows a scene where Ino had been represented crying for her intentions against Themisto's children.

Athamas' and Ino's crimes against their own children are joined in the reconstruction by Welcker, where they are narrated by a *deus ex machina* at the conclusion of the play, in accordance with what is referred to in Hyginus' *Fabula* 4. In other reconstructions, Athamas' killing of Learchus is separated from Ino's actions in the Melicertes' episode. In Hartung's proposal, the chorus tries to persuade Ino (who had already sent Learchus to accompany Athamas in hunting) not to commit suicide. In all proposals, it is the announcement of Learchus' killing in a messenger's speech that precedes. In his proposal, Hartung thinks that Learchus' body was brought on stage. This idea is also accepted by Jouan and van Looy, who suppose that Athamas himself carries the dead corpse of Learchus, just as Agave carries her son Pentheus' head in the *Bacchae* (1168–1215). As regards the representation of Ino's episode with Melicertes, scholars usually think that there is room only for Ino's flight from stage with her young son in her arms. In all proposals, therefore, Ino's subsequent suicide with Melicertes and their deification are thought to be narrated by a god (usually Dionysus) in a *deus ex machina* scene at the end of the play.

Separation of Ino's mania from that of Athamas is something not implied in Hyginus' *Fabula* 4.[13] Thus, it could be considered as the personal idea of some scholars (except Welcker), if it had not been recently confirmed by the text of the *Oxyrhynchus Papyrus* 5131, from which we can safely understand that a child is being carried dead in front of Athamas and immediately followed by Ino's lament. Moreover, in all reconstruction proposals two elements are arbitrarily excluded. The first is Ino's maenadic flight to Cithaeron, which is given

---

[13] Separation here refers to the onstage representation of Athamas' and Ino's mythical madness. This is different from what Slater 1968:405 says about the uniqueness of the mythological example of Athamas' and Ino's mania in that they are of different sexes and behave differently, while other mythical persons, who are driven mad together, are treated as one case.

a big part in Hyginus' *Fabula* 4 but is not included in any of the reconstruction attempts. The second is the reference in Euripides' *Medea* 1282–1289 to Ino's murder of both her children in a state of mania,[14] which could be thematically connected (as a motive of the maenadic Ino) with her maenadic wander in Cithaeron, narrated in Hyginus' *Fabula* 4, even if in the *Medea* Hera is mentioned as the goddess who inspires mania in Ino rather than Dionysus.

2.3 Reconstruction Problems

Adapting the *Oxyrhynchus Papyrus* 5131 to Hyginus' *Fabulae*

With these data, the text most important to the reconstruction of the play becomes the newest papyrus fragment, the *Oxyrhynchus Papyrus* 5131. P. Finglass showed that the text must have come from Ino's lamentation scene, on top of a child's lifeless body, in the presence of Athamas.[15] For this scene, Finglass determines the details very accurately: before Ino's lamentation, the dead body is carried to the stage by servants, perhaps with Athamas as their guide, and placed before Ino for her impending grief.[16]

Finglass's proposal, which identifies the child's body as Learchus, Athamas' and Ino's eldest son, is based primarily on the last—the shortest—part of Hyginus' *Fabula* 4, where it states that Athamas killed Learchus in a state of madness.[17] But, the greatest part of Hyginus' *Fabula* 4, as I have already noted, consists of Ino's exit as a maenad in Cithaeron, her return to the house of Athamas, and her secret cohabitation with Themisto as a servant, which frame Themisto's tragic filicide; Athamas' madness (in which he killed one of his and Ino's sons, Learchus), as well as Ino's (who leaped into the sea with her other son, Melicertes, and was then deified), is presented very succinctly at the end of Hyginus' narrative in a manner that could evoke a *deus ex machina* delivery of the events at the end of the play.

If now we attempt to combine Hyginus' narrative with the papyrus passage, which establishes as certain the transfer to the stage of the child's dead body before Athamas and Ino, and the resulting lamentation of the latter, the plot described above would probably be arranged as follows: prologue (by Athamas or Ino); parodos (by the chorus); first episode (a confrontation between

---

[14] See in the Commentary (Chapter 1).

[15] Finglass 2014:69–70.

[16] Finglass 2014:70–76.

[17] Finglass 2014:70–71 argues that in his *Fabula* 8 Hyginus makes a similar assertion in the case of Antiope and her name play by Euripides; and his summary of Euripides' *Antiope* matches well the extant fragments of the play.

Athamas and Themisto); first stasimon (by the chorus); second episode (Ino's and Themisto's conspiring); second stasimon (by the chorus); third episode (murder of Themisto's children with Ino's plotting); third stasimon (by the chorus); fourth episode (a messenger speech of Athamas' madness, the murder of Learchus, and possibly the restoration of Athamas' sanity); fourth stasimon (by the chorus); fifth episode (the arrival of Athamas with the body of his child on stage, Ino's lamentation); fifth stasimon (by the chorus); exodus (narration by a *deus ex machina* of Ino's suicide with Melicertes and her divine transformation); the chorus' exodus.

The pattern that inevitably arises disrupts the immediate succession of Athamas' madness (the murder of Learchus) and also Ino's (the Melicertes episode), which exists in Hyginus' *Fabula* 4. Finglass admits that the papyrus fragment presents a disruption in the unity of Athamas' and Ino's act of madness, and he maintains that this disruption, which also appears in Ovid *Fasti* 485–502 (particularly 489–494),[18] does not apply to the tragicality of Ino, who led other children to their death in order for her to save her own, and now she witnesses the death of her son at the hands of his father.[19] However, when implemented, this disruption of unity in Athamas' and Ino's madness enhances the dramatic plot of the play with four additional scenes and the killing of one more child. I am in agreement that, as a dramatic event, Learchus' murder and the lamentation for him thereafter provides powerful substance to the tragicality of the scheming Ino, but this mitigates the tragic murder of Themisto's children,[20] which makes up the main event in Hyginus' narrative. As for the increase in killings, Finglass accurately observes that the papyrus fragment itself indicates this with the pronoun ἄλλη (in verse line 3), and provides the murder of little Astyanax in the *Trojan Women* as an example.[21] Yet, in the *Trojan Women*, the murder of little Astyanax does not disrupt the tragic unity of the play because it is carried out by the victorious Achaeans who were responsible for all the atrocities resulting from the fall of Troy. In that case, the murder of Hector's young son heightens the *hybris* in the victors' behavior. On the contrary, Ino's lamentation on the body of her son disrupts the tragic unity of the play because it shifts the tragic focus from Themisto's filicide to Ino's punishment, mitigating the amount of pain from the preceding double murder of Themisto's children. Moreover, this does not comply with the main line of the tragedy that Hyginus'

---

[18] See the comments by Littlewood 2006:154–157. Cf. Parker 1999.

[19] Finglass 2014:76. For Ino's maddened situation when she kills her son Melicertes, see McHardy 2005:135.

[20] For example, in Sophocles' *Antigone* Eurydice's suicide, which is announced by a messenger, does not detract from the previous double suicide of Antigone and Haimon; instead, it increases their tragic importance.

[21] Finglass 2014:72–73.

narrative follows (Themisto's filicide and suicide). And, in addition, all of the unanswered questions that Finglass himself poses relative to Athamas' madness (if he had ever returned to sanity) and Ino's guilt (saving her own children in the place of Themisto's) remain.[22]

In a later article, Finglass attempts to approach these problems with the idea that Euripides' *Ino* is a unique play, whose unity is maintained by the distinct character of the title heroine. The key tragic motifs are female jealousy,[23] failure of recognition,[24] and kin killing,[25] which ensure consistency in the play through repetition.[26] Thus, it is necessary that Ino becomes the moral instigator in the murder of Themisto's children and to then endure the pain from the murder of her own children, at least Learchus.[27] From this perspective, the Euripidean *Ino* surpasses even the *Medea.*[28] Moreover, it depicts Athamas, having lost four children, as more tragic a hero than Jason, who lost two.[29] With this very interesting proposal, Finglass adapts the thematic analysis of the *Ino* to the reconstruction problems that arose from the papyrus fragment, the most important of which is the accumulation of murders. The examples that Finglass provides from other tragedies ensure the tragicality of the themes of kin killing[30] and jealousy.[31] However, it is not certain that these examples are sufficient in addressing the dramatic plot of the four child murders, which remain unique to the plot of the *Ino.* Regarding Ino's moral responsibility for the killing of Themisto's children, Finglass thinks that it was "an essentially defensive tactic"[32] in order to save her own children. He also thinks that Ino feels regret, thus acknowledging her moral responsibility.[33] The idea of Ino as exceptionally tragic, as a double filicide, is a welcome theme. But, apart from Ino's lamentation, which is confirmed to be the climactic event in the play,[34] the dramatic scenes that Finglass discusses here are mainly the restoration of Athamas' sanity and his lamentation for Learchus,[35]

[22] Finglass 2014:74–76.
[23] Finglass 2016:305.
[24] Finglass 2016:307.
[25] Finglass 2016:303–304.
[26] Finglass 2016:308.
[27] Finglass 2016:309–310.
[28] Finglass 2016:303.
[29] Finglass 2016:312–315.
[30] Finglass 2016:303–305.
[31] Finglass 2016:305–306.
[32] Finglass 2016:309.
[33] Finglass 2016:310–311.
[34] Finglass 2016:303.
[35] Finglass 2016:312.

which he himself submitted earlier as part of the restoration.[36] Perhaps we need a trial in applying this idea to the play's entire plot.

What is especially interesting is Finglass's reference to Chapter 14 of Aristotle's *Poetics* (1453b14–1454a13),[37] which distinguishes between four types of kin killing in ancient tragedy. Finglass claims that the example of the Euripidean *Ino* can be placed in the third category (unwittingly killing kin and the realization thereafter), which Aristotle characterizes as superior (βελτίονα) but not best (κρατίστην). However, the chapter in the *Poetics* can provide us with different ways in which to approach the reconstruction of Euripides' *Ino*. I will therefore convey the most important points. First, I must mention Aristotle's willingness to provide an example for each of the cases he discusses. But an example respective to the third category, which would have suited the Euripidean *Ino*, if we were to assume that the murder of the children happened unwittingly, as Finglass showed, is absent. Furthermore, Euripides' *Ino* is nowhere mentioned in the paragraph, even implicitly. The first thought is that Aristotle did not know the play. Yet, Euripides' *Ino* would have been well known in Aristotle's time (fourth century BCE), since it was of interest until late antiquity;[38] so, it is not very probable that it would have escaped his attention. The next thought is that kin killing in Euripides' *Ino* does not fall within Aristotle's criteria. If this were the case, I observe that the instances that Aristotle lists do not include kin killing under the influence of madness.[39] In all instances, Aristotle's criteria are based solely on the awareness or ignorance of the dramatic persons in respect to the circumstances surrounding the murder they commit. However, awareness, as well as ignorance, are preceded by various degrees of sanity on the subject's behalf, but madness means the breakdown of mental function. Therefore, kin killing committed under the influence of madness perhaps does not quite fit the criteria that Aristotle establishes as the basis for his examinations. And the absence of a reference to Euripides' *Ino* rather implies an absence of a variation in mental states as a criterion for the interpretation of Ino's actions in the play. Moreover, Hyginus' *Fabula* 4, which describes Ino's involvement in the murder of Themisto's children, does not correlate to any of Aristotle's criteria that would qualify Ino as a tragic heroine. Quite the contrary, Aristotle's criteria designate Themisto (the mother who unwittingly killed her own children) as the tragic

---

[36] Finglass 2014:74–75.

[37] Finglass 2016:304n12.

[38] Finglass 2016:315.

[39] Among the extant tragedies, mad killings appear in Euripides' *Heracles* and *Bacchae*; and they are both filicidal. In fragmentary tragedies, mad killing (filicide) occurs, for instance, in Aeschylus' *Lycurgeia* trilogy, where Lycurgus kills his son in madness. In the *Lycurgeia* trilogy and the *Bacchae* madness is inspired by Dionysus; in the *Heracles* it is expressed with Dionysian wording (119 Ἄιδου βάκχος).

heroine. Consequently, the placing of Themisto in a position as a secondary heroine, as Finglass suggests, is not made simple.[40]

Methodologically, I agree with Finglass in that Hyginus' *Fabula* 4 is the only text from antiquity that refers directly to the Euripidean *Ino* and thus we are obligated to take it seriously into consideration. On the other hand, the papyrus text is more credible scientifically, which ensures the characters and the elements of its content. Finglass ultimately admits that Hyginus' narrative does not provide the foundation for the dramatic events of the triple murders that the papyrus fragment presents; and he exalts the importance of the papyrus text by arguing for "a master tragedian," who would find a way to move from the heartless to *flebilis* Ino. As an example he brings the figure of Clytemnestra who "receives such distinct portrayals, and such differing levels of sympathy, in different dramas, even though the basic details of the plot (she kills her husband and mistreats her surviving children) remain unchanged."[41] Yet, it is rather difficult to think of any real difference in the levels of sympathy that the tragic figure of Clytemnestra receives in different dramas, since in most cases she remains an awful figure. For instance, in Aeschylus' *Agamemnon*, Clytemnestra's claims for the sacrifice of her daughter, Iphigenia, don't extinguish her guilt; and it is not certain that in the *Libation Bearers* Clytemnestra becomes pitiful when she begs Orestes to respect her and not kill her. In my opinion, the contradictions that the papyrus fragment generates in relation to Hyginus' narrative do remain under investigation, making it questionable to adopt his *Fabula* 4, especially its ending, whose credibility has long been debated.[42] Therefore, I shall seek a solution through a faithful reading of the papyrus and pursue elements with a high degree of reliability that could be included in Hyginus' mythographic narrative.

I shall begin with the papyrus text. In the Commentary I have noted that in verse line 8 the accusative personal pronoun νιν, which Finglass read as accusative singular, could in fact be read as accusative plural. If this were the case, then Ino's lamenting does not occur over one dead body (Learchus'), but more, in this case, two: Learchus' and Melicertes'; cf. Sophocles *Antigone* 577 μὴ τριβὰς ἔτ', ἀλλά νιν / κομίζετ' εἴσω, δμῶες, where νιν refers to both Antigone and Ismene. This hypothesis is reinforced by the possibility that the word ψυχά in verse line 12 is the Attic form of the dual nominative (/accusative/vocative) ψυχά (for two persons), referring to the souls of Athamas' two murdered

---

[40] Finglass 2016:311.

[41] Finglass 2016:309.

[42] Bursian 1866:776; Schmidt 1872:40; Wilamowitz-Moellendorff 1931–1932:1.218n3; Luppe 1984; disagreement (with Bursian and Schmidt) by Rose 1933. Certainly, Wilamowitz's cautiousness about *deus ex machina* scenes in Euripides' early plays has been removed by the new papyrus fragment of Euripides' *Ino*; see Finglass 2014:72n55.

children.[43] In addition, it is not necessarily right that the perfect participle λεληθώς (in verse line 11) refers to the dead. It may very well have Athamas as its subject who in devastation asks (in first person singular) for the funeral pall to be pulled so that he could see with his own eyes that under the pall are his children (to never forget the murder of his children).[44] As I argued in the Commentary, this is the meaning of the verb λέληθα when it is used with an infinitive, and the syntactical conjunction of the verb λέληθα with an infinitive cannot be excluded from this particular passage. The events would then better correlate to Ino's filicide, which would confirm Ino's tragic lamenting over the body of her children. With this version, the madness of Athamas is no longer an issue. On the contrary, Athamas would have been informed or would have himself discovered the murder of his children and either follows or guides the transference of their bodies to the stage before their mother. In addition, the version that I describe is almost identical to the reference made to Ino's filicide by the chorus in the *Medea* (1282–1289). If Ino is in fact a child murderess, she would have had her logic restored in the previous scene, followed by a messenger speech by Athamas, that would announce the return of Ino's logic. Almost instantly, Finglass's previously mentioned questions are resolved. What then remains is Ino's suicide, which could have been announced in narration by a *deus ex machina* at the end of the play.

The biggest objection to my hypothesis is, of course, the fact that in Hyginus' *Fabula* 4 the filicide that is spoken of is Themisto's. On the other hand, we must not overlook that what is clear in the narration of *Fabula* 4 are Ino's actions, beginning with her role as a maenad in Cithaeron, continuing with her role as an anonymous servant, and culminating in her participation in the act of filicide: as Themisto's trusted servant, Ino secretly changes the garments of the potential victims, saving her own children from the murder that was being plotted against them by the jealous Themisto who commits the last tragic filicide. Ino's connection to attempted filicide exists in other narratives, which refer to Ino's act against Phrixus and Helle, Athamas' children from his first wife Nephele. However, in those narratives, Ino is a plotter rather than a murderess. What is evident though is that in those narratives Ino operates rationally, in full knowledge of the consequences, and shows no signs of madness. Namely, she appears as a non-maenad.

---

[43] See in the Commentary *ad loc.* (Chapter 1).

[44] Cf. Sophocles *Ajax* 1003 (ἴθ', ἐκκάλυψον ὡς ἴδω τὸ πᾶν κακόν), where Teucer arrives ordering Tecmessa to uncover Ajax's body so that he may see the worst; Euripides *Hecuba* 679–680 (ἀλλ' ἄθρησον σῶμα γυμνωθὲν νεκροῦ, / εἴ σοι φανεῖται θαῦμα καὶ παρ' ἐλπίδας), where a servant girl, carrying the body of Polydorus, urges Hecuba to uncover the corpse to mark the body now laid bare, (in order to see) if it is a sight to fill her with wonder and upset her hopes.

By now reviewing the total presentation of the mythical Ino, we discover that two items are unique: a) the reference of Hyginus' *Fabula* 4 to the heroine's maddened (maenadic) state (fleeing from the house of Athamas to Cithaeron and her forced return to him) and b) the reference in Euripides' *Medea* to the filicide by Ino in a state of mania. The uniqueness of these two items, which are linked to the subject of Ino's madness, allows us—I would suggest in the next chapter—to methodologically search for elements of madness that have a true connection to Euripides' *Ino*. The fact that Hyginus dedicated a separate narrative to Euripides' *Ino*, and wrote yet another narrative about Ino (*Fabula* 2), is significant; and it is significant, too, that the case of *Fabula* 4, where this particular tragedy is referred to separately, is unique to the entire mythographic work of Hyginus.[45] Both factors are at least indicative that the Euripidean tragedy *Ino* had a special composition. If indeed the Euripidean version were considered acceptable, the time period until Hyginus' era (second century CE) was more than sufficient for its dissemination and prevalence. But it appears that, even in Hyginus' time, the composition of the *Ino* would have been considered neoteric and probably remained unique, a fact that would compel Hyginus to add *Fabula* 4 to his narratives, particularly for Euripides' play. Additionally, the surviving papyrus text is later than Hyginus' narrative with a possible dating in the beginning of the third century CE. According to Finglass's convincing explanation, the papyrus text must have come from some teaching of the *Ino*, possibly in Oxyrhynchus, at the beginning and not end of the third century CE, and is perhaps among the last performances of Euripides' work in antiquity. This possibility increases the likelihood that Euripides' *Ino* remained known for its uniqueness and was chosen to be among the works of Euripides taught till late antiquity.

---

[45] Hyginus' *Fabula* 8 (*Eadem Euripidis quam scribit Ennius*), referring to Euripides' *Antiope*, has a different purpose; thus, it may be read in different terms, as I will explain in Chapter 3.

3

Interpretation Matters

3.1 Ino's Mania

From a Nurse of Dionysus to a Jealous Wife: Hera's Manifestation of Mania

The relationship of Ino with Dionysus appears as a literary matter at the early fifth century BCE. In Homer, Ino is mentioned as Cadmus' daughter, with the added detail that her mortal nature later became deified through her transformation into a water goddess under the name of Leucothea:[1]

> τὸν δὲ ἴδεν Κάδμου θυγάτηρ, καλλίσφυρος Ἰνώ,
> Λευκοθέη, ἣ πρὶν μὲν ἔην βροτὸς αὐδήεσσα,
> νῦν δ' ἁλὸς ἐν πελάγεσσι θεῶν ἒξ ἔμμορε τιμῆς.

> Homer *Odyssey* 5.333–335

> But the daughter of Cadmus, Ino of the fair ankles, saw him, even Leucothea, who of a mortal of human speech, but now in the deeps of the sea has won a share of honor from the gods.[2]

In Hesiod's *Theogony*, Ino is the first of the four daughters to be mentioned that Harmonia bore to Cadmus (975–977), but there is no mention of her deification, though the poet mentions Semele's deification elsewhere after her union with Zeus and the birth of Dionysus:

> Καδμείη δ' ἄρα οἱ Σεμέλη τέκε φαίδιμον
> μιχθεῖσ' ἐν φιλότητι, Διώνυσον πολυγηθέα,
> ἀθάνατον θνητή· νῦν δ' ἀμφότεροι θεοί εἰσιν.

> Hesiod *Theogony* 940–942

---

[1]   For Ino-Leucothea, see Farnell 1916 and 1921:39–47; Finkelberg 2006.
[2]   Translation by Murray 1919.

Semele, Cadmus' daughter, mingling in love, bore him a splendid son, much-cheering Dionysus, a mortal woman giving birth to an immortal son; and now both of them are gods.[3]

As a nurse to Dionysus, Ino is mentioned for the first time in Pherecydes (FGrHist 3F 90=Fowler F 90cd), in a passage where the Hyades are mentioned. There, it states that the Hyades were the first to nurse Dionysus as the Nymphs of Dodona and accompanied him on his wanderings as a giver of wine, but Lycurgus' pursuit of Dionysus and their fears of Hera forced them to entrust Ino with his upbringing.[4] From Pherecydes' narrative, an archetype of Dionysus' nurses emerges, who come in the form of archetypal maenads: they roam with the god—still an infant—to save what he worships (wine). In that image of the archetypal maenad are the elements of wandering and pursuit, but not (yet) mania, which was not a part of infant-Dionysus' worship (since he offered wine). So when Ino receives Dionysus from the prototypical nurses, she simultaneously acquires the characteristics of his worship. She becomes the archetypal nurse and companion to Dionysus and would monitor Hera's vindictive tendencies, as the Hyades did before her.[5]

In the later Apollodorus' narrative (*Library* 3.4.3),[6] Dionysus is given to Ino (and Athamas) by Hermes and not the Hyades. Therefore, any link of Ino to the archetypal elements of the nurse is eliminated.[7] However, there are other details that point to the theme of mania that do not appear in Pherecydes' narrative; more specifically, Hera's display of madness, which encompasses the hallucinations of both parents, Athamas and Ino; Athamas kills their eldest son while hunting, mistaking him for a deer,[8] and Ino boils their youngest son before falling into the sea. So, I think that in the narrative of the earlier Pherecydes, Ino's role as nurse to Dionysus is an archetypal feature, which is then supplemented with behavioral characteristics that are associated with the madness of

---

[3] Translation by Most 2006.

[4] Fowler 2013:372; he disbelieves in the wine cult of the baby Dionysus and thinks it more likely that it was Ino who gave Dionysus to the Hyades. But, even in that case, Ino's care of young Dionysus is not disputed. Moreover, the tradition of Pherecydes' text is valid.

[5] In extant literature, Ino is not fully established as a nurse of Dionysus before Ovid *Metamorphoses* 3.313, 4.421, 524, *Fasti* 6.485. In extant Greek literature, the earlier references are found in Plutarch *Aetia Romana* 17 (267e) τὸν ἐκ τῆς ἀδελφῆς ἐτιθηνήσατο; Pausanias 3.24.4f [Prasiai] ἀποφαίνουσι μὲν τὸ ἄντρον ἔνθα τὸν Διόνυσον ἔθρεψεν Ἰνώ. For Ino as the archetypal maenad, see Henrichs 1978:137–143, especially nn61–62.

[6] See in Chapter 2.

[7] The Nymphs are κουροτρόφοι by nature; see West 1966 *ad* Hesiod *Theogony* 347.

[8] In Apollodorus' narrative one may also pay attention to hunting as an element of Dionysiac cult, which is prominent in Euripides' *Bacchae*, especially in Agave's scene (1153–1210) where Dionysus is called her partner in hunting (1145–1146 ... ἀνακαλοῦσα Βάκχιον / τὸν ξυγκύναγον, τὸν ξυνεργάτην ἄγρας).

the god. In this way, we go from the archetypal nurse to the maenad of Dionysus, so that the archetypal model of the nurse and Bacchic madness merge. Hera was used as an established mythological link because of her known hostility towards Zeus' illegitimate sons. Additionally, what is particularly interesting about the narrative is that the manifestation of mania by Hera is associated with filicidal acts, considering that Athamas and Ino each killed one of their children. In the *Library* we also have the first mythography of the relationship between Ino and Athamas' children from other marriages (1.9.1–2), which I have described in Chapter 2. In this narrative, too, the mythographer completes the recounting of Athamas' fate with the enraged Hera, without indicating the reason behind her divine wrath. The components of Hyginus' *Fabula* 2 are more or less the same, with the noteworthy exception of Phrixus' willingness to be sacrificed, the details of which I will discuss later in this chapter.

Features of the mythological versions that I have described above can be found in some scanty fragments of all three major tragedians. In particular, Ino's maniacal act at the expense of the younger Melicertes perhaps existed in Aeschylus' *Athamas* (TrGF 3 F1–4a), in two of the fragments that mention a cauldron with boiling water (frr. 1, 2a). This event would constitute a powerful showing of Ino's mania, that when performed would consolidate the theatrical image of the maddened heroine. More examples of the madness that Hera inflicted upon Ino and Athamas might also have existed in one of the two *Athamas* tragedies of Sophocles; however, the few and scant fragments that exist do not give us insight into this matter (TrGF 4 F 1–10). In Sophocles' second *Athamas*, which includes a scene involving Nephele's children, there was probably no room left for the unfolding of Hera's mania, because, according to preserved texts, the most impressive scene in that play is the one in which Athamas wears a wreath, and is led to be sacrificed after the escape of Phrixus and Helle, but is later saved by the arrival of Heracles.[9] Of these scant fragments, one suggests Dionysus with a reference to an abundance of wine (fr. 5 οἴνῳ γὰρ ἡμῖν Ἀχελῷος ἆρα ναι) and the second depicts a redemptive atmosphere (fr. 6 λευκὴν ἡμέραν), possibly after the hero had been saved.[10]

Better than the quantity of material in the fragments proves to be their depiction of the two same-titled *Phrixus* tragedies of Euripides. However, in none of their surviving fragments is there a reference to Hera or to Ino's (and Athamas') madness. The *Oxyrhynchus Papyrus* 3652 (Column 2.16–31) has led to the assumption that these plays shared the same myth (according to *Hippolytus A*

---

[9] Scholia *ad* Aristophanes *Clouds* 257; cf. testimonia in TrGF 4, pp. 99–100.

[10] Ancient lexicographers show a festive atmosphere (fr. 6 λευκὴν ἡμέραν: ἡδεῖαν καὶ ἱλαράν, ἢ ἀγαθὴν καὶ ἐπ᾽ εὐφροσύνῃ); see the citations in TrGF 4 F 5, 6. So, Sophocles' *Athamas B* might have been produced in the position of a satyr play.

and *Hippolytus B* of Euripides), which was centered around Ino's plotting against Nephele's children, with Euripides' creative adaptation in presenting a Phrixus who voluntarily sacrifices himself when he learns of Ino's supposed oracle.[11] In a version like this, there would be little opportunity to include Ino's and Athamas' madness except in a *deus ex machina* scene that would tell of Hera's vindictive act through narration.

Hyginus' *Fabula* 2,[12] which also refers to Phrixus' voluntary sacrifice, must therefore have some Euripidean *Phrixus* as its source. This narrative states that a servant, who takes pity on Phrixus, reveals the identity of the scheming Ino to Athamas, causing Athamas to deliver Ino and little Melicertes to Phrixus so that he would kill them; but Ino is saved by the intervention of Dionysus. Hera then induces Athamas' madness, causing him to kill Learchus, while Ino falls into the sea with Melicertes. This narrative, which appears to represent the mythical Ino (by having the title *Ino*), is consequential to my subject, because it involves Dionysus as Ino's protector; moreover, it depicts the heroine as Athamas' victim, since her fall into the sea appears to be in an escape from Athamas' madness (cf. Dionysus' escape into the sea in Homer *Iliad* 6.130–137). Hyginus' *Fabula* 2 is akin to Euripides' *Ino* in her relationship to Dionysus. Thus, I assume that in his *Phrixus* tragedies, Euripides upholds the Aeschylean version of Ino's madness by presenting the connection between the heroine and Dionysus dramatically. But what seems even more pertinent is the predating of the *Phrixus* tragedies to the *Ino*; in those plays, Euripides first shows Ino's and Dionysus' primordial relationship, and then later moves on to convert the heroine into his maenad.

One more piece of evidence seems to be of special interest. In 415 BCE the tragic poet Xenocles was the winner at the Great Dionysia (against Euripides) with the plays *Oedipus, Lycaon, Bacchae,* and *Athamas* (TrGF1 33 F1), which means that Xenocles' *Athamas* was presented as a satyr drama after his tragedy entitled *Bacchae.* It is difficult to imagine which elements of Athamas' fate were possible for parody in the plot of a satyr play. Otherwise, we must suppose that Xenocles presented his tragedy *Athamas* in the place of the satyr drama as Euripides had done with his *Alcestis* in 438 BCE. In that case Xenocles could confirm the Dionysian spirit of his tetralogy with Ino as a wife of Athamas, dramatizing her relevance to Dionysus, especially her Bacchic agency. It is thus also important that the tragic poet Achaeus from Eretria, a specialist in satyr plays, composed a tragedy entitled *Phrixus* (TrGF1 20 F38). In any case, the fate of Athamas' children was rather interesting for tragic poets, especially Aeschylus' offspring,

---

[11] Webster 1967:131–136; he argued that *Phrixus A* was about Phrixus' adventures in Colchis.
[12] See Chapter 2.

since his nephew Philocles wrote a tragedy entitled *Phrixus* (TrGF1 86 T3),[13] and in the fourth century (341 BCE) a tragedy entitled *Athamas* was composed by Astydamas (TrGF1 60 F1), Philocles' grandson (and Aeschylus' great-grandson).

Nonnus (in the fifth century CE) produced a poetic composition of mythological data in an extensive epic narrative about Dionysus (*Dionysiaca* 9–10), which is not a mythographic, but a literary work. Here, too, Nonnus states that Hera's wrath stems from Semele's mockery and from Ino's agreement to raise little Dionysus with the condition that she be transformed into a sea goddess. Hera's vengeance towards Ino as Dionysus' nurse takes the form of the aforementioned madness, which transforms Ino into a maenad and leads her in a maddened state to Parnassus, from where Apollo eventually takes her (9.243–286). Athamas who then—in vain—sought Ino, marries Themisto who bears him two children, Orchomenus and Sphingius. Themisto, who in rivalry wants to kill Ino's children, kills her own children by mistake, believing them to be Ino's (9.319–321). Ino, having returned after a three-year absence, finds Athamas in a maddened state, which then evolves into the traditional mythic narrative (Learchus, Melicertes) of Ino's suicide by falling into the sea (10.67–125). In Nonnus' poetic composition, the influence of Euripides' *Ino* is evident, as we know from Hyginus' *Fabula* 4. But, there is one difference worth noticing: Nonnus' Ino is not involved in the murder of Themisto's children. With a newfound freedom in poetic composition,[14] the later Nonnus is probably able to preserve Ino's maenadic quality, while separating it from the murder of Themisto's children. In that case, Hyginus' *Fabula* 4 could perhaps have played a critical role in avoiding confusion between the maenadic versus jealous child-murderess, since the dramatic status of the jealous filicide mother was claimed—I would suppose—exclusively by the Euripidean Medea.

3.2 Ino as a Maenad

As I previously noted, the tragedy entitled *Ino* can be ascribed only to Euripides and its only remaining source is Hyginus' *Fabula* 4. In the case of Ino, *Fabula* 4 differs mainly in its link of Ino with the Dionysian maenadism on Cithaeron, which includes the trait of plotting. In its core event, the filicide, Hyginus' *Fabula* 4 presents a stark similarity to his *Fabula* 1 (entitled *Themisto*), where Themisto's filicide is also described. There, Ino is referred to as the third wife of Athamas, who simply causes Themisto's rivalry, while the role of the plotter belongs to an anonymous nurse who dresses Themisto's children as the targeted victims

---

[13] The information that the play was composed by the comedian Timocles, who also wrote tragedies, is not proven; maybe this is another Timocles, a tragic poet.

[14] For Nonnus' liber fantasy, see Slater 1968:284n10.

because she pities Ino. This similarity, if examined more closely, is fundamental and is significant because not only is the filicide of Themisto's children the same, but also the role of the plotting female (changing the clothes of the targets).[15] Only the role of the nurse from *Fabula* 1 does Ino assume in the *Fabula* 4. As for her position relative to the knowledge of those involved, as much so in *Fabula* 1 as in *Fabula* 4, the fated nurse, who saves Ino's children from murder, is in the service of Themisto, whom she trusts. However, the difference between the two narratives is encountered in the characterization of Ino as maenad, which exists only in *Fabula* 4. These traits must have also been specific to Euripides' *Ino*, to which *Fabula* 4 specifically refers. And I mention that Ino's filicide, to which the chorus in the *Medea* (1282–1289) refers, results from madness with the key characteristic of wandering that belongs mostly to maenadism. Of course, the chorus in the *Medea* attributes Ino's madness to Hera and not Dionysus. But the same is true in the *Heracles*, where Heracles' imminent madness, which is also induced by the vindictive Hera, is conveyed by the Bacchic atmosphere of the lyric exchange between the chorus and his father, Amphitryon (indicatively 889–900 κατάρχεται χορεύματ' ἄτερ τυπάνων / οὐ Βρομίου κεχαρισμένα θύρσῳ), and adequately summed up with the characterization of him as a *Bacchos* of Hades, after his filicidal act (1086 ἄν' αὖ βακχεύσει Καδμείων πόλιν, 1119 εἰ μηκέθ' Ἅιδου βάκχος εἶ, φράσαιμεν ἄν). Therefore, we have the right to proceed with the hypothesis that, with the tragedy *Ino*, Euripides innovated by presenting Ino killing her own two children in madness. If Euripides' innovation in the *Ino* was only the identity of the intriguing person (Ino instead of an anonymous female servant), Hyginus probably would not have written a specific narrative for the play.

In my opinion, Euripides' reinvention of the *Ino* could have had its beginnings in the mythological version of the filicidal Themisto, who kills her children unwittingly as the result of the nurse's fated act in favor of Ino (as Hyginus' *Fabula* 1 describes). Euripides, who was perhaps more interested, as I have already explained, in the idea of Ino as a maenad, altered the existing mythological

---

[15]   In the scheme of Themisto, where the bright robes of Ino's children were exchanged for dark ones, we may discern elements of sacrificial ritual. In the *Heracles*, the children are also dressed in funeral costumes for their doom ordered by Lycus (329 κόσμον πάρες μοι παισὶ προσθεῖναι νεκρῶν, 442–443 ἀλλ' ἐσορῶ γὰρ τούσδε φθιμένων / ἔνδυτ' ἔχοντας, 525–526 ... τέκν' ὁρῶ πρὸ δωμάτων / στολμοῖσι νεκρῶν κρᾶτας ἐξεστεμμένα); the same also happens in the *Melanippe Sophe*. On the other hand, on many occasions (in tragedy) dark clothes are associated with lament (e.g. *Alcestis* 425–427 and 922–924; *Helen* 1087–1088 and 1186–1187; *Phoenissae* 325–326; *Orestes* 456–458; Aeschylus *Libation Bearers* 1012–1013) while bright clothes are associated with celebration (*Phoenissae* 323–324 δακρυόεσσ' ἀνεῖσα πένθει κόμαν; Aeschylus *Eumenides* 352 παλλεύκων δὲ πέπλων †ἄμοιρος† ἄκληρος ἐτύχθην). So, Hyginus' reference to the exchange of the costumes of Themisto's children may be thought of as valid, despite the objections by Webster 1967:100.

narrative of the filicide Themisto by emphasizing elements of maenadism. So, he made Ino a maenad of Dionysus, identified her as the anonymous nurse (who pitied her in *Fabula* 1), and made Ino unwittingly kill her own children in a state of Bacchic mania while participating in the revenge actions of the jealous Themisto. With this adaptation he also gave a new dramatic substance to the already existing tradition of Hera's vindictive mania through the filicide that Ino and Athamas shared between them. Consequently, we are obliged to investigate and explain which of the elements in Hyginus' *Fabula* 4 are authentic and which have undergone mythographic alterations, since mythographers had the organization and clarification of mythological material as their main objective; in other words, they may have also served as the copiers of manuscripts, adding, removing, or correcting elements they believed to be irregular, especially if they did not have the original texts at hand and instead acquired their content from a synopsis (a Hypothesis in the case of tragedy).[16]

Per prevailing literary opinion, for the composition of his *Fabula* 4, Hyginus had a Hypothesis of Euripides' *Ino* and not the work itself.[17] Based on the information in *Fabula* 4, this Hypothesis must have certainly stated that the Euripidean Ino became a maenad in Cithaeron, and that Athamas returned her secretly to his house, and placed her in the service of his new (third) wife Themisto. However, if Hyginus knew the mythological version of Themisto's filicide (narrated in his *Fabula* 1), while the Hypothesis of Euripides' *Ino* (which he had in his hands) referred to Ino's filicide and her subsequent suicide (as it is described in the *Medea* 1282–1289), he would have become skeptical of the information in the Hypothesis, especially if it were too concise. Therefore, with the idea that the author (probably anonymous) of the Hypothesis could have made a mistake in the identity of the perpetrator (he wrote Ino instead of Themisto), Hyginus may have chosen to proceed with the rationalization of the alleged abnormality and corrected the Hypothesis of the Euripidean *Ino*, based on his more familiar mythological version, that of the *Fabula* 1 (*Themisto*).

Through his rationalization of the myth, Hyginus had omitted the most basic element of the Euripidean *Ino*, the heroine's act of filicide. In this way, he could proceed with the completion of the work's plot by relaying its one common theme, the vengeful wrath of Hera, especially since the abbreviated Hypothesis, which he had as his guide, may not have included it. Nevertheless, the same conclusion also appears in *Fabula* 2 (*Ino*), the one which represents the archaic Ino. If we examine it more closely, the reference made to Hera's mania at the

---

[16] Rose 1930:36–42 (for Hyginus); Huys 1996 and 1997. Cf. Slater and Cropp 2009:78; Marshall 2009. Already Dietze 1894 had acknowledged that the only manuscript of Hyginus, now lost, was an impeccable Latin translation of a Greek mythographic work.

[17] Luppe 1984.

end of *Fabula* 4 does not reveal the identity of the goddess Hera (who causes the madness); it rather appears to include details of the manifestation of her mania that are missing at the end of *Fabula* 2: that Athamas' madness emerged while he was hunting, that Learchus, whom Athamas killed, was the eldest son, and Melicertes, with whom Ino fell into the sea, was the youngest. For this reason, the reference to Hera's vengeful wrath at the end of *Fabula* 4 cannot be considered a reliable authentic component of the Euripidean *Ino*, but a marginal annotation that found its way into the text of Hyginus' *Fabula* 4. Analogous is the case of *Fabula* 32 (entitled *Megara*), which is inspired—fortunately—by a surviving play, Euripides' *Heracles*. Hyginus there changed the unorthodox ending of Euripides' play (asylum in Athens offered by Theseus to the murderous Heracles) with a more orthodox version (that of Heracles' wrath against Apollo, who refused to give him purification from his heinous murders).[18] Hyginus' aim there is not to arrange different versions of Heracles' purification, but to eradicate unorthodox inventions by the poets about the theme. So, the fact that he has not written a specific narrative for Euripides' *Heracles* indicates that the crucial dramatic event of the play (the murder of Heracles' wife Tecmessa and his children) was not mythically strange—as Ino's filicide may have been—and that prompted him to write the specific narrative of *Fabula* 4.

The example of the specialized mythographic narration of tragedy is repeated by Hyginus in his *Fabula* 8, under the title *Eadem Euripidis quam scribit Ennius*. This narrative refers specifically to Euripides' *Antiope* and follows his *Fabula* 7, entitled *Antiopa*, which more generally refers to the mythical Antiope. Yet their actual components, when compared to Hyginus' narration about Ino, are not similar. The narratives about Antiope complement each other with isolated details from the same myth,[19] without resulting in a conclusion that the Euripidean *Antiope* had a different myth from the known mythological rendition.[20] Therefore, the idea that Hyginus' *Fabula* 8 can be confirmed by the surviving fragments of Euripides' *Antiope* has only a relative value. Nonetheless, the main purpose of the title of *Fabula* 8 itself (*Eadem Euripidis quam scribit Ennius*) is to relay that the *Antiopa* by the Latin poet, on whom the interest is focused,

---

[18] In his *Fabula* 31.20-25, Hyginus gives a different version of Heracles' purification: *Neleum Hippocoontis filium cum decem filiis [Hercules] occidit, quoniam is eum purgare sive lustrare noluit tunc cum Megaram Creontis filiam uxorem suam et filios Therimachum et Ophiten interfecerat* (He [Heracles] killed Neleus son of Hippocoon and ten of his children because he was not willing to cleanse or purify him after he killed his wife, Megara daughter of Creon, and his sons, Therimachus and Ophites); see Rose 1933:42.

[19] Huys 1996:173.

[20] See the fragments of Euripides' *Antiope* in TrGF 5.1 F179-224; especially the long *Flinders Petrie Papyrus* (fr. 223), which preserves a part of the end of the play.

has precisely the same content as Euripides' *Antiope*,[21] without it implying that Euripides' *Antiope* has subversive differences from the existing mythological tradition of its heroine, as has occurred with Euripides' *Ino*, about which Hyginus was compelled to write in *Fabula 4*.[22]

---

[21] Hyginus' mention of Ennius is mistaken because it is Pacuvius, not Ennius, who wrote a tragedy named *Antiope*. Finglass 2014:71n39 rightly thinks that the additional phrase *quam scribit Ennius* in the title of Hyginus' *Fabula* 8 is probably a marginal annotation by a reader of the text, who may have misremembered Cicero *De Finibus 1.4 Ennii Medeam aut Antiopam Pacuvii.*

[22] See Huys 1996:173. Against Huys's "excess" skepticism argued Cameron 2004:45–46, who is accepted by Finglass 2014:71n42.

4

Reconstruction Proposal

4.1 Reconstruction Attempt

Following the above discussion, I believe I can proceed with my reconstruction proposal for Euripides' *Ino*. From Hyginus' *Fabula* 4, I mainly question the identity of Themisto in the act of filicide, as well as the reference to Athamas' and Ino's madness by Hera as events in the play for the reasons I have stated, especially in Chapters 2 and 3. Instead, I find the reference to Ino's maenadic status (which is indicated primarily in the mentioning of Cithaeron) of major importance, because it does not exist anywhere else. Meanwhile, I accept that the reference to Ino as a filicide in Euripides' *Medea* is powerful evidence *ante quem*, because it presupposes the audience's relevant knowledge in order for it to be grasped, and the knowledge could not have existed if the chorus were referring to an unknown version of the myth.[1] Owing to available information that suggests a reinvention of Ino by Euripides himself, I am led to believe that the Euripidean *Ino* belongs to the poet's plays prior to the *Medea*, where the novelty of his Ino is invoked by latent self-referentiality. Ino's novel situation (madness and filicide) becomes the center of her adaptation in the *Medea*, while it simultaneously diverges from the powerful image of Ino as a Dionysian maenad to the familiar mythological origin of her madness from Hera.

Of the surviving texts, the most recent, the *Oxyrhynchus Papyrus* 5131, adds new information, which requires consideration in the reconstruction of the play. Due to the papyrus text, we have as certain two dramatic events, probably from the end of the *Ino*: a) Athamas bringing a child's body before Ino; and b) Ino's subsequent lamentation for the dead, which would provide her with an exceptional tragic moment only if the murder of her child was a crucial,

---

[1]   See Newton 1985; in his opinion, there is not an innovation by Euripides, but an intentional "mistake" of the chorus, which was designed to shake the audience for Medea's infanticide to be received as unparalleled. But Newton's argument, concerning audience response, presupposes readiness—if not ability—of the spectators to understand the deeper meaning of a deliberate mistake by the poet.

not a supplementary, event of the play. Finglass rightly observes that "Ino's song over Learchus' body provided the drama with a moment of great pathos, an emotionally intense aria delivered by a figure who might have been one of Euripides' most memorable female characters."[2] The papyrus also establishes as certain the onstage presentation of the restoration of the killer in sanity and makes it impossible that the filicide was narrated in a *deus ex machina* scene at the end of the play. Therefore, in reconstructing the *Ino*, we must consider that the surviving book fragments—which are mainly gnomological—could fit in a scene of Ino and Athamas' devastation and/or of the heroine's lamentation. Furthermore, the content of a *deus ex machina* scene at the end of the play could not include the news of at least one of Ino's children's murder. These factors are highly significant because it is then possible to reconsider many of the older reconstruction proposals,[3] which also differ and/or contradict each other in the placement of an individual fragment, and only one of them (the proposal by Hartung) foresees the transfer of the deceased Learchus to the scene.

From the indirect evidence, the first two data are found in the contemporary comedy. The satirical comment of Aristophanes' *Acharnians* about Ino's rags is one criterion—perhaps an obvious one—for the dramatic role of the heroine as a servant to Themisto. Yet, it may have also been referring to Ino's maenadic appearance. Nevertheless, if Ino's filicide did indeed occur, her tattered clothing would have truly captured the heroine's impoverishment, particularly in her mourning scene. I find the second satirical account of Aristophanes in the *Wasps* (1412-1414) to be even more insightful, where he comments on Ino's pale face, that it hangs from the legs of Euripides. It is known that this passage has had various interpretations, primarily as an indication of a supplication scene of Ino pleading to Athamas.[4] However, the comment should be interpreted in light of the metaphorical use of the word hanging, in the spirit of the idea first introduced by A. Matthiae and pushed further by other scholars.[5] In other words, it means that the image of Ino's despair and fear hang from Euripides. Such a trial on the poet's behalf could be discussed, if it were indeed true that the chorus in the *Medea* alluded to Ino killing her children. In that case, Ino's filicide, under the control of divine fury, would be a powerful mitigating factor in the heroine-plotter's guilt and could have provoked Aristophanes' comment on the appropriateness or effectiveness of Euripides' dramaturgical choices.

If Hyginus' narrative is not mistaken, the dramatic space of the play would have been Thessaly. The plot would have started in the typical manner of a

---

2 Finglass 2014:76
3 See in Chapter 2.
4 See in the Commentary *ad loc.* (Chapter 1).
5 Matthiae 1829:196.

Euripidean prologue. In his monologue, in all likelihood, Athamas would have first reverted back to Ino's fleeing to Cithaeron and his subsequent marriage to Themisto. He would then explain his undertaking to bring Ino home after finding her in Cithaeron, as well as the choice to place her among the servants of the palace and conceal her identity from Themisto. The fragment 398 could have summarized the new—and difficult—situation by using the wording of sleep metaphorically: Ino's new situation is a trouble that was asleep for a long time (εὕδουσα δ' Ἰνοῦς συμφορὰ πολὺν χρόνον) and now opens its eyes threateningly (νῦν ὄμμ' ἐγείρει). One might think of the maenads' awaking up in Euripides' *Bacchae* in the first messenger's speech, where the maenads become dangerous (731–764) after their waking up (692–693 αἱ δ' ἀποβαλοῦσαι θαλερὸν ὀμμάτων ὕπνον / ἀνῇξαν ὀρθαί). It is worth noticing that Finglass, who attributes this fragment to an unknown drama,[6] thinks that Ino's εὕδουσα συμφορά might refer to her former flight to Cithaeron, where she worshipped Dionysus.[7]

The mental status of the maenad-Ino, after her return from Cithaeron, will be analyzed with respect to the later Agave of the *Bacchae*, who fails to recognize her victim, her son Pentheus (1118–1124), but is able to communicate rationally about all other circumstances: she remembers the existence of her father and son (1211–1215) and she immediately recognizes Cadmus (1233) when he appears on stage with the dismembered parts of the lacerated body of Pentheus. She then remembers—and asks that it be performed with great accuracy—the entire ritual for her success as a hunter: to hang the prey above the palace entrance and organize a formal dinner (1239–1243). A similar type of communication about things can also be supposed in the case of the maenad Ino. For the expediency of the drama, the only thing that Ino would not recognize is her children.

One scene—probably from the first episode—would have shown the grim prospects of the maenad Ino's return to her former home. The heroine, addressing the chorus (fr. 399) of women (φίλαι γυναῖκες), would have expressed her inability (πῶς ἄν ...) to renounce her maenadic ways (τῶν πεπραγμένων δράσασα μηδέν) and resume a domestic role in the palace of Athamas (ἐξ ἀρχῆς δόμους Ἀθάμαντος οἰκήσαιμι). As I mentioned in the Commentary, Plutarch's interpretation refers to Ino's remorse for her past deeds, which could be none other than Ino's plotting against Phrixus and Helle.[8] However, Hyginus' *Fabula* 4 leaves no room for memory or prior involvement in her plotting against Phrixus and Helle in the story of Euripides' *Ino*. Hyginus instead placed the plotting in *Fabula* 2 (*Ino*), from which he makes a cautious distinction in *Fabula* 4 (*Ino*

---

[6] Finglass 2016:300n3.
[7] Finglass 2014:71, even with his own criteria.
[8] Welcker 1839–1841:2.618; cf. Finglass 2016:305–306.

Euripidis). The "other life," in the words of Plutarch, is domestic life, to which, in my opinion, Ino's Bacchic orgia in Cithaeron could be opposed (cf. *Bacchae* 32-38, 443-446, 513-514, 700-702).[9]

In a dialogue between her and Athamas, following her address to the chorus, Ino would have responded in maenadic negativity to the erotic appetite of her former spouse, who in fact wants her to be his secret second wife (frr. 400, 401). In fr. 400 Ino cries for women's concerns (ὦ γυναικεῖαι φρένες) by cursing Aphrodite (Eros/Love) as a disease (ὅσον νόσημα τὴν Κύπριν κεκτήμεθα). In fr. 401 she loudly protests women's unhappiness against that of men (ὅσῳ τὸ θῆλυ δυστυχέστερον γένος πέφυκεν ἀνδρῶν) and argues that female sex is left far behind in good times, and yet further in bad (ἔν τε τοῖσι γὰρ καλοῖς πολλῷ λέλειπται κἀπὶ τοῖς αἰσχροῖς πλέον). Ino's vigorous protests maybe ironically combined with elements of sophist ideas about monogamy and polygamy spoken by Athamas. In fr. 402 laws in force are accused (νόμοι γυναικῶν οὐ καλῶς κεῖνται πέρι) for their monogamic content: facing only one wife (εἰς μίαν βλέπουσι), men take a great risk (κίνδυνον μέγαν ῥίπτοντες), because they do not test manners of their brides before they ballast them in their houses (οὐ γὰρ τῶν τρόπων πειρώμενοι νύμφας ἐς οἴκους ἑρματίζονται βροτοί). The idea is that a prosperous man would be right to have as many wives as possible (χρῆν γὰρ τὸν εὐτυχοῦνθ' ὅτι πλείστας ἔχειν γυναῖκας), provided that he would have food for all of them in his house (εἴπερ τροφὴ δόμοις παρῆν). Thus, he could throw the bad wife out of his home and keep the one who is actually good (ὡς τὴν κακὴν μὲν ἐξέβαλλε δωμάτων τὴν δ' οὖσαν ἐσθλὴν ἡδέως ἐσῴζετο). These verses probably belong to a speech by Athamas, arguing for his decision to marry Themisto after Ino's flight to Cithaeron.[10] Having been unwillingly transferred from Cithaeron by Athamas and become Themisto's secret servant, Ino suffers misfortune. In fr. 406 she asks Athamas not to scowl so much at her misery, because he is human too. And she would supply her reminder by a *sententia*, in accordance with her powerless situation. In fr. 407 it is probable Ino who condemns harshness and thriftiness, if one sheds no tears for those suffering pitiful misfortunes and does not benefit anyone though he has enough money.

Moreover, Ino would be sympathetic to Themisto. Thus, in a dialogue between them, in the second episode, some fragments could be included that refer to the unhappiness Ino feels and to Themisto, the queen, consoling her for

---

9 Webster 1967:100 thinks that τῶν πεπραγμένων (in the fragment) may refer to what Ino committed in *Fabula* 4 itself; from them her maenadic deeds in Cithaeron, which are firstly referred to in Hyginus' narrative, should not be excluded (in my opinion).

10 Of course, neither Ino nor Themisto could be excluded as speakers; each one could claim against Athamas' polygamy in a strong ironic way. In the case we suppose that the speaker is Ino, we have to transmit fr. 402 in a dialogic scene between her and Themisto probably in the next (second) episode.

it with moderate *sententiae* (frr. 418, 408, 409). In fr. 418 Themisto counsels Ino to understand the human condition and not feel pain beyond measure, since she is not the only person who lies in misfortunes. Themisto encourages Ino to be hopeful about life (fr. 408), though she balances her admonition with an austere diction about *hybris*: not to slacken reins in bliss (fr. 409).[11] In her answer, Ino admits human misfortunes as a rule with a gnomological idea: that the cycle is the same for mankind and earth's fertile plants. Some people enjoy wealth while the life of others falls into decay and is harvested again (fr. 415).[12] And, recounting in secret Athamas' marital situation, she pushes her idea further by attributing audacity (*thrasos*) to those who are silent about their misfortunes (in that case, Athamas' unhappy marriage to Themisto) and try to conceal their troubles (fr. 416). Themisto then continues with the wish to have a poor—worse than a beggar—friend, who will be faithful to her so that he (/she) will overcome fear and speak the language of his (/her) heart (fr. 412).[13]

Debates would have then ensued between the two women, based on the general disadvantaged state of women as well as the demands of marriage. In fr. 414 Themisto would urge Ino to take care of noble men but disdain the bad ones as they deserve. In her answer (fr. 422) Ino would refer to Athamas' untrustworthiness by paradigmatically mentioning his Thessalian descent. Ino could therefore have contributed to Themisto's jealous reaction, especially if Themisto had targeted Athamas, since she did not know her servant's true identity. In fr. 410 Themisto would approve the courage of Ino's convictions by saying that, as a wife, she deserves to have a maid who will not be silent about worthy things and feels hate for what is shameful without concealing it from her eyes. From her own part, as a privileged servant, Ino would express her loyalty to her mistress with *sententiae* that declare her authority in nobility and wisdom. In fr. 413 she appears to recite characteristics of her noble birth: to keep silence where necessary and speak where safe, to see what she ought to and not to see what is not proper, and to control gluttony. All these declare—and confirm—her liberal manners, despite her current servitude. Themisto thus trusts Ino and asks her to be silent about their agreement, which needs to be kept secret from all citizens (fr. 411).

During Ino's participation in Themisto's act of jealous revenge, the element of maenadic obscuration would have been applied to the victims' identity, as I

---

[11] For the connection of fr. 409 with fr. 418, see Hartung 1843:1.460.

[12] The reaction of the maenadic Ino to accepting Themisto's consolation is different from the reaction of other Euripidean grieving characters, who appear unreceptive to the admonition addressed to them (Karamanou 2017:164 on *Alexandros* fr. 5). See Chong-Gossard 2016 for irony in manipulation of consolation by Euripides.

[13] The masculine gender of the words in the text is in line with the general nature of the opinion expressed here about friends, which does not exclude friendship to refer to a woman.

have explained above. Ino would have been involved in the murder of her children without being able to recognize them. In this way, Ino's madness would have been the bearer of tragedy in this drama. The murder would have taken place in the palace. Some servant would have discovered it, and/or Athamas himself, who would have announced the event in a narrative speech (in the third episode), explaining that Ino's madness did not allow her to recognize her children.[14] Fr. 403 could have come from this speech, where the speaker would have expressed his horror of female jealousy and envy with exclamatory questions, wondering what mother or father bore the ill-named envy as a great evil for the human race. The following references to current medical procedures (surgery, medical remedies) along with anatomical details about parts of the human body (3–7) are better to be understood as a means of ironically expressing the horror of the aroused situation, which is undisputable otherwise. In Athamas' same speech there could have been a reference to Themisto's ethical or actual guilt in condemnation of female jealousy. Even if in the *Ino* we rank Themisto in a secondary position, since we consider the title heroine to be the central character of the play, it is Themisto, Athamas' jealous wife, who organized the murder of her rival's, Ino's, children.[15]

The continuation of the dramatic events requires the restoration of Ino's sanity. For this endeavor, perhaps Euripides' *Heracles* shows us the way.[16] After announcing the murder, Athamas confronts Ino and reveals the details of the gruesome act until she grasps what happened in reality. Immediately after, the *Oxyrhynchus Papyrus* 5131 text is placed.[17] At the end of the third stasimon, the chorus announces the entrance to the scene of the servants who are carrying the dead bodies of the children. The weight is small for the servants but ἀλγεινόν (unbearable) for their father, who asks for the bodies to be cautiously placed. Particularly, commenting on οἱ π[έλας at verse 8, Finglass considers οἱ as an article, and reads οἱ πέλας as "a strange designation for the corpse-bearers, who are approaching the palace rather than stationed nearby."[18] But, as I have already mentioned in my comment *ad loc.*, οἱ could also be a dative of the third-person personal pronoun, to be precise, a feminine gender dative, referring to

---

[14] Athamas' grief for the murder of his children would be too great to be reported by a messenger in a third person speech; see Finglass 2014:74n68.

[15] For the secondary position of Themisto, see Finglass 2016:311–312. Fr. 403 is perhaps unsuitable to be attributed to (the lamenting) Ino, because the heroine would have appeared to denounce something that she herself, even unwittingly, had partaken in.

[16] We might also recall Agave's recovering to sanity with the help of her father Cadmus in the *Bacchae* 1233–1326; since, in my proposal, the corpses of the dead children are in the palace, we may overcome the cautiousness by Finglass 2014:74n69.

[17] See the text in the Commentary (Chapter 1).

[18] Finglass 2014:74n62.

Ino. In that case, Athamas would indicate to the servants to place the corpses beside Ino. Athamas could himself be at the head of the procession leading the children's bodies to their mother for the awaited lamentation. However, I find it preferable to integrate the events of the scene into one (the fourth) episode, where we are now towards the last part of the play.[19] In other words, Athamas would not have left to rejoin and guide the servant's ritualistic procession, but would have remained on stage, waiting with the now rational Ino, for the children's bodies to be carried in. He would have interceded with a small choral ode that would have ended in the announcement of the five anapests.

Athamas' brief apostrophe towards the servants, in only four iambic trimeters, has raised some questions: Had he already seen and lamented for his children in the palace, or is it the first moment he faces them? If the second instance is true, when will he lament his children?[20] I believe that in the preceding speech (in the third episode), where he announces the filicide, there was enough opportunity for him to express his pain,[21] and show remorse for his own responsibility in the situations that were created as a result of his polygamy and his violent behavior toward Ino the maenad. As I have previously stated, fr. 403 is quite indicative of Athamas' position, who in a state of shock expressed his horror of the dangers of female jealousy. In a new scene (in the fourth episode), the father's pain is demonstrated in a ritualistic act. Athamas requests the ceremonial uncovering of the bodies before the lamentation.[22] The horrible spectacle robs him of his speech, which now belongs to the mother of the children who unwittingly committed the murder. The silent presence of Athamas through Ino's lamenting was one way to participate in the mourning.[23]

The condition of the papyrus in the section dedicated to Ino's lamenting does not allow for the formulation of even one phrase. However, the verbal clues are sufficient to secure the contents of this scene.[24] Therefore, in Ino's

---

[19] Finglass 2016:301.
[20] For the possibility of lament by Athamas, see Finglass 2014:73n61; cf. Finglass 2016:302. For male laments, see Suter 2008 (Finglass 2014:75n78). The fact that in archaic paintings men are associated with the more formal manifestations of mourning as opposed to the women's passionate grief (Alexiou 2002:6) does not mean that they were excluded from the threnos of the dead. See Koonce 1962 for formal lamentation in tragedy.
[21] Perhaps in an epirrhematic exchange between Athamas and the chorus (e.g. Sophocles *Ajax* 348–429). Finglass 2016:302 thinks that Athamas might also participate in the mourning of his wife Ino.
[22] The papyrus (in verses 10–11) includes elements of funerary ritual, especially in the use of peplos, for which see in the Commentary *ad loc.* (Chapter 1).
[23] In Sophocles *Ajax* (974–1039), Tecmessa watches in silence Teucer's long lament over the corpse of Ajax immediately after her own threnos. In Euripides' *Ino* too, Athamas' lament might have been performed shortly before Ino's mourning.
[24] Finglass 2014:75n70.

lamentation we can assume that there is a place for the gnomological passages in fragments 404 and 405, in which the heroine would express with tragic prudence her contemplations about the eugenic expectations that parents have from their marriage (that the noble born will dominate earth, fr. 404); particularly, she would rationalize her expectations of her children's well-being by claiming that nobility, even if a marriage is inadequate, is held in honor by many people, who prefer to acquire it for their children's sake (fr. 405). It is worth noticing that in fr. 405 the prevalent verb is προσλαβεῖν, which means gain. At the end of the lamentation passage, we could also place fr. 421. Although this fragment could describe Athamas as self-exiled (*emigré*) in dark desolation after the murder of his sons, I prefer Ino as the speaker with the arguments I brought in the Commentary *ad loc*. Ino would either damn Athamas[25] wishing for his exile to wild places (like a beast, alone)[26] or prepare for her own exodus (suicide) to escape to the solitude of the darkness of Hades (in hollow caves without any lighting torches). In the second case, Ino appears to compare her escape to a wild animal in the mountains, like the images of a wild maenad (e.g. *Bacchae* 982 λευρᾶς ἀπὸ πέτρας).

I would place the remaining gnomological fragments in a *deus ex machina* speech, which would have most likely been given by Dionysus. In this speech, the god of madness would have foretold of Ino's fortune: the immediate suicide of the heroine by leaping into the sea and perhaps also her transformation into a sea goddess, according to known mythological facts.[27] This possibility is enforced by Athenagoras *Legatio* 29.4 (ὁπότε καὶ Ἰνὼ μετὰ τὴν μανίαν καὶ τὰ ἐπὶ τῆς μανίας πάθη θεὸν δοξάζουσι γεγονέναι "πόντου πλάνητες Λευκοθέαν ἐπώνυμον" καὶ τὸν παῖδα αὐτῆς "σεμνὸς Παλαίμων ναυτίλοις κεκλήσεται"), where Ino's catastrophic mania is distinguished from her own and Melicertes' deification. In that occasion, we might include in the *Ino*'s fragments the two anonymous verse lines cited by Athenagoras (TrGF 2 F 100–101 πόντου πλάνητες Λευκοθέαν ἐπώνυμον/σεμνὸς Παλαίμων ναυτίλοις κεκλήσεται).[28] As a *deus ex machina*, Dionysus would have been gnomological with respect to the guilt of Athamas, to whom he would have attributed abuse of wealth and power (frr. 419,

---

[25] Cf. *Medea* 160–165, the lamenting Medea's curses against Jason, his new bride, and the royal house.

[26] Cf. Apollodorus *Library* 1.9.2 (in Chapter 2), where, at the end of his adventures, the exile Athamas builds his own country, the Athamantis, in a land of wild animals (wolves).

[27] For deification of Ino and Melicertes, see Pache 2004:135–180; Finglass 2007 (on Pindar *Pythian* 11.2); Kowalzig 2013:52.

[28] These verses were attributed to Euripides' *Ino* by Wilamowitz 1893:26 (= Wilamowitz 1935–1972:1.201), who later became doubtful about Hyginus' narrative concerning the end of the play, let alone that Wilamowitz didn't know the (new) papyrus text, which enhances our distrust of the end of Hyginus' *Fabula* 4. See also Wilamowitz 1935–1972:2.21n40.

417, 420), as well as an indifference to the plight of the weak (such as *flebilis* Ino in this drama and the betrayal of Themisto).

In fr. 419 Dionysus would condemn violence through which wicked men draw honors and pursue for wealth with actions just and unjust mixed together, but at the end they reap an unhappy harvest from them. In fr. 417 the god would endorse mankind to acquire rightly what they need and preserve it by keeping themselves far from blame; meanwhile they should honor everyone who deserves their respect and not behave like a bad sailor, who, having once been fortunate, seeks more and more, and then loses everything. In fr. 420 Dionysus would offer the example of the tyrants, who lose their strength, though long increased, by slight lapses; one day may overthrow some from a height and elevate others; wealth especially has wings and flies so that those who once had it, being frustrated in their hopes, fall on their backs.

In such a plot reconstruction, proposed for Euripides' Ino, the situations that arose pertain to the theme of female jealousy and filicide as its means of expression. And this tragic component is realized through divine intervention, since the heroine's madness comes from a goddess (Hera) and is expressed by the means of the god of mania (Dionysus).[29] That is why the children's murder, in the way it happens, would also function as an instrument of divine vengeance against Athamas for isolating Ino from her maenadic duties, which would alter the mythological guilt of the hero, who was usually considered to accept the consequences of Hera's fury merely as the spouse of Ino, nurse to Dionysus.

4.2 Comparison with Euripides' *Medea*

The proposed events of the Euripidean Ino raise the theme of conjugal fidelity and female jealousy in a neoteric way. If we accept the Ino's myth as it was presented above, the play becomes a predecessor to the Medea, which was also composed in a new style, the foreign bride of Colchis becoming a filicidal heroine to avenge Jason's infidelity. Mythologically, Medea could be linked to the Athamantides through Phrixus: she is the daughter of the King Aeetes of Colchis, to whom Phrixus gave the golden fleece. But more significant is her possible connection to Ino, nurse of Dionysus, according to the ancient Hypothesis of the Medea, where, among the magic acts of the heroine, it states that she rejuvenated Dionysus' nurses and their husbands after having baked them.[30] But what is most important about this information about Medea's actions is that it regards the lost work of Aeschylus' *Nurses* or *Nurses of Dionysus* (Τροφοί/Διονύσου Τροφοί), probably a

---

29 For a list of Hera's victims, Mattes 1970:37–38.
30 See Mills 1980, for similarities and differences between Ino's and Medea's (as well as Procne's) story. Cf. Fontenrose 1948.

satyr play (TrGF 3 F 246a 3–5 Αἰσχύλος δὲ ἐν {ταῖς Διονύσου} Τροφοῖς ἱστορεῖ ὅτι καὶ τὰς Διονύσου τροφοὺς μετὰ τῶν ἀνδρῶν αὐτῶν ἀνεψήσασα [ἡ Μήδεια] ἐνεοποίησεν).[31] Thus, in these magical processes, we are justified in including Ino, as the archetypal nurse of Dionysus and eponymous wife of Athamas.

Beyond her magic performances, the pre-Euripidean Medea is also linked to the act of filicide, though unintentional. The occurrence relates to the love of Zeus, whom Medea rejected in order to escape Hera's wrath. As a reward, Hera promised to make Medea's sons immortal. In the story that Eumelus (fr. 8 Bernabé) narrates, the heroine put her children through some sort of trial, but, instead of making them immortal, she inadvertently causes their death.[32] In Euripides' *Medea*, she kills her children intentionally, to make her revenge towards Jason more potent. The idea of Medea's deliberate filicide, as a tool to slander the heroine, is included in Didymus' narration, which paraphrases Creophilus' story. Medea murdered Creon and fled to Corinth, leaving her young children in the sanctuary of Heraion of Pechacora for protection where they were found and killed by Creon's relatives (Scholia *ad Medea* 264). It appears that Euripides was familiar with this narrative because in the *Medea* 1303–1305, after the murder of Creon and Glauke, Jason comes to save his children from the vengeance of the dead king's relatives. The poet likely merged the two narratives of Eumelus and Creophilus, designating Jason's infidelity as the motive for murder.[33] The intentional vengeance is also present in the filicide in the *Ino*, even in Hyginus' version in *Fabula* 4, since Themisto seeks revenge on Athamas with the murder of Ino's children, who were also his, though unaware of the true identity of her victims.

As a rational filicide, the Euripidean Medea shows no signs of madness, despite the horror of her act. Furthermore, it has been correctly noted that Bacchic vocabulary is absent from the heroine's language, although Dionysiac patterns are used metaphorically for kin killing, especially in Euripides' plays.[34] I will pause only at the moment that Medea expresses the idea to murder her children. The idea was not part of a premeditated plan, nor was it a decision that was already made but was concealed by the heroine up until that very moment. Precisely, the idea of filicide enters suddenly into Medea's mind (790 ἐνταῦθα μέντοι τόνδ' ἀπαλλάσσω λόγον), when she completes her plan to murder Glauke

---

[31] Similar actions of Medea were also known in relation to Jason or/and his father Aison, by Pherecydes (FGrHist 3 F 113) and Simonides (PMG 548); TrGF 3 F 246a 1–3 Φερεκύδης δὲ καὶ Σιμωνίδης φασὶν ὡς ἡ Μήδεια ἀνεψήσασα τὸν Ἰάσονα νέον ποιήσειεν. περὶ δὲ τοῦ πατρὸς αὐτοῦ Αἴσονος ὁ τοὺς Νόστους ποιήσας φησὶν οὕτως. See Graf 1997.

[32] Scholia *ad* Pindar *Olympian* 13.74; Pausanias 2.3.7–11; Scholia *ad* Lycophron *Alexandra* 174–1026.

[33] This interpretation school for Euripides' voluntary murder Medea holds from Page 1938. For the myth of the Corinthian Medea, see Johnston 1997.

[34] See Schleiser 1993:57–114; Seaford 1993:129–133, especially 132n84.

and Creon. It is a momentary lapse of reason resulting from an extreme vengeful passion. As such, it could be compared to a sudden bout of madness. However, the dramatic direction of the play does not leave room for irrational action. This is why Medea's first response to her lapse of reason is to cry (791 ᾤμωξα δ' οἷον ἔργον ἔστ' ἐργαστέον). Yet she instantaneously turns an irrational or demented idea into a rational process, and incorporates it into her plan, eliminating all traces of madness:

791   ᾤμωξα δ' οἷον ἔργον ἔστ' ἐργαστέον
        τοὐντεῦθεν ἡμῖν· τέκνα γὰρ κατακτενῶ
        τἄμ'· οὔτις ἔστιν ὅστις ἐξαιρήσεται·
        δόμον τε πάντα συγχέασ' Ἰάσονος
795   ἔξειμι γαίας, φιλτάτων παίδων φόνον
        φεύγουσα καὶ τλᾶσ' ἔργον ἀνοσιώτατον.
        οὐ γὰρ γελᾶσθαι τλητὸν ἐξ ἐχθρῶν, φίλαι.
        . . . .
        οὔτ' ἐξ ἐμοῦ γὰρ παῖδας ὄψεταί ποτε
        ζῶντας τὸ λοιπὸν οὔτε τῆς νεοζύγου
805   νύμφης τεκνώσει παῖδ', ἐπεὶ κακὴν κακῶς
        θανεῖν σφ' ἀνάγκη τοῖς ἐμοῖσι φαρμάκοις.

Euripides *Medea* 791–806

Ah me, I groan at what a deed I must do next. I shall kill my children: there is no one who can rescue them. When I have utterly confounded the whole house of Jason, I shall leave the land, in flight from the murder of my own dear sons, having committed a most unholy deed. The laughter of one's enemies is unendurable, my friends. . . . . . He shall never from this day see his children by me alive, nor will he beget children by his new bride since that wretch must die a wretched death by my poisons.[35]

In my opinion, Euripides' adaptation involved the elimination of the elements of irrational decisions from Medea's filicide. In this way, Medea's filicide is a decision that was taken in the course of the plot, while the heroine's vengeful plan was unfolding.[36]

---

[35] Translation by Kovacs 1994.

[36] Finglass 2014:75n73 pays attention to the fact that, apart from Medea's lyric anapests heard from inside the palace early in the play (*Medea* 96–167), there is not any lyric ode (or/and lament) by the heroine till the end of the drama, despite its terrible events.

This element is one more factor that defines the relationship between the Euripidean Ino and Medea. The maenadic attribute is a critical difference between Ino's and Medea's filicide. Therefore, if we accept that the tragedy *Ino* was produced before the *Medea*, we can maintain that Euripides progressed dramatically from the status of an archetypal maenad to the image of a conscious filicide, disassociating the latter from an act of madness. This finding is significant to the dramatic art of the poet, because in his tragedies following the *Medea* what he increasingly employs in order to identify horror actions is Bacchic vocabulary, which implies characteristics of madness belonging to the god Dionysus himself. As I have already mentioned, in the *Heracles*, a tragedy that did not come long after the *Medea*, the title hero becomes unnecessarily and unintentionally an uxoricide and filicide from the madness that Lyssa instills in him through the ordering of the jealous Hera. However, the placement of Heracles' impending fury within a Bacchic framework (878–879, 889, 966, 1142), as well as his characterization as a *Bacchos* of Hades (1119), indicate that the content of the hero's action should be dramatically understood as a Dionysian one.[37]

The complete absence of Bacchic vocabulary from Medea's act in her name play of Euripides makes the heroine unique in ancient tragedy in terms of the role that consciousness plays in the criteria of human action. The subject is an intellectual one that characterizes the thoughts of the sophists of that time. The Euripidean Ino and Medea constitute two poles that define with equal tragicality the role of consciousness in human action. Medea's filicide is extremely emotional, a result of a powerful vengeful passion. Ino's participation in Themisto's vengeance is also emotional, as a manifestation of revenge towards Athamas. However, the absence of rational knowledge in the identification of the victims is the element that shows the abysmal difference between rational and irrational sentiment.[38] The madness of the god of theater was intended to express its corresponding action. The other, the rational tragedy, does not belong to his vocabulary. That is why the Euripidean Medea is unique.[39] The tragic model of Medea the filicide arose from the archetypal model of Ino maenad-nurse of Dionysus, also unique so that its repetition would be impossible.

---

[37] See the detailed quotations by Schlesier 1993: 94nn24, 25 for all three major tragedians.

[38] Padel 1995:208, notes that "the worst, strangest thing about Medea is that she is *not* mad." For this difference between Ino and Medea, see Papadopoulou 2005:62–63. It is true that in the ancient comparison between Medea and Ino by Horace (*De Arte Poetica* 123 *sit Medea ferox invictaque, flebilis Ino*) madness is not applied as a criterion; nor is it excluded. As it appears, Horace's comparison arises from the scenes at the end of the two plays. The image of the wild and victorious Medea recalls her flying on Helios' chariot while Ino's *flebilis* image can be connected with Ino's threnos attested by the new papyric fragment, as Finglass 2014:75n78 supposes.

[39] Newton 1985:501–502 argues for the uniqueness of Medea's filicide with the idea that Ino's killing of her children was intentionally invented by Euripides.

5

Text and Translation

Prologue

> fr. 1 (*398 Kannicht)
>
> ΑΘ(ΑΜΑΣ)
>> εὕδουσα δ’ Ἰνοῦς συμφορὰ πολὺν χρόνον
>> νῦν ὄμμ’ἐγείρει
>
> ATH(AMAS). Though for a long time asleep, Ino's misfortune now awakens and opens her eye.

Schol. Pind. *Isth.* 4.39a ἰδοῦσα δ’-ἐγείρει | Plut. *Antony* 36.1 εὕδουσα δ’ ἡ δεινὴ συμφορὰ χρόνον πολύν ‖ 1 εὕδουσα . . . συμφορά Musgrave, Welcker 618: ἰδοῦσα . . . συμφοράν Schol. | πολὺν χρόνον Schol.: χρόνον πολύν, Nauck²

> Parodos
> . . . .
> First Episode

> fr. 2 (**399 Kannicht)
>
> ΙΝ(Ω)
>> φίλαι γυναῖκες, πῶς ἂν ἐξ ἀρχῆς δόμους
>> Ἀθάμαντος οἰκήσαιμι τῶν πεπραγμένων
>> δράσασα μηδέν;
>
> INO. Dear women, how is it possible to live from the beginning again in Athamas' home as if I did nothing of what I did before?

Plut. *De sera numinis vindicta* 11 (556a)

fr. 3 (400 Kannicht)

IN.   ὦ θνητὰ πράγματ', ὦ γυναικεῖαι φρένες·
ὅσον νόσημα τὴν Κύπριν κεκτήμεθα

INO. Oh, peoples' dealings! Oh, hearts of women! How great is the afflic-
tion of Aphrodite, which we have acquired!

Stob. 4.22.183 ‖ 1 γυναικεῖαι: γυναικείας A

fr. 4 (401 Kannicht)

IN.   φεῦ,
ὅσῳ τὸ θῆλυ δυστυχέστερον γένος
πέφυκεν ἀνδρῶν· ἔν τε τοῖσι γὰρ καλοῖς
4   πολλῷ λέλειπται κἀπὶ τοῖς αἰσχροῖς πλέον

INO. Alas! How much more miserable the female gender is by nature
than that of men! For, in the good times it is at a disadvantage and in
the bad even more.

Stob. 4.22.182 ‖ 3 ἔν τε τοῖσι γὰρ καλοῖς: ἔν τε γὰρ τοῖσι<ν> καλοῖς? Blaydes 1902,
244 ‖ 4 κἀπὶ : κἄτι? Blaydes 1894, 1.1

fr. 5 (402 Kannicht)

ΑΘ.   νόμοι γυναικῶν οὐ καλῶς κεῖνται πέρι·
χρῆν γὰρ τὸν εὐτυχοῦνθ' ὅτι πλείστας ἔχειν
{γυναῖκας, εἴπερ τροφὴ δόμοις παρῆν},
4   ὡς τὴν κακὴν μὲν ἐξέβαλλε δωμάτων,
τὴν δ' οὖσαν ἐσθλὴν ἡδέως ἐσῴζετο.
νῦν δ' εἰς μίαν βλέπουσι, κίνδυνον μέγαν
ῥίπτοντες· οὐ γὰρ τῶν τρόπων πειρώμενοι
8   νύμφας ἐς οἴκους ἑρματίζονται βροτοί

ATH. The laws in force are not properly made concerning woman-
kind. For, a prosperous man should have as many wives as possible,
{provided that there would be sufficient wealth in his home to feed
them}. In that case, he would drive the bad woman out of his house and
willingly keep the one who is actually good. Now, however, men look

to one wife, at their own great risk. For, people drive brides like ballast into their houses, without having any experience of their ways.

Stob. 4.22.36 ‖ 2 ὅτι Stob. 4.22.36: ὅπως Erfurdt | ἔχειν Stob.: γαμεῖν Nauck²: τρέφειν Headlam ‖ 3 del. Mekler: εἴπερ <ἂν> τροφὴ δόμοις παρῆν Schwyzer 2.350: εἴπερ <δὴ> τροφὴ δόμοις παρῆν Stob. ms. Paris 1985: εἴπερ <ἡ> τροφὴ δόμοις παρῆν Gesner, Cropp: εἴπερ <ἐν> δόμοις τροφὴ παρῆν Pflugk: εἴπερ δώμασιν τροφὴ παρῆν Nauck¹.

fr. 6 (406 Kannicht)

IN.   μὴ σκυθρωπὸς ἴσθ᾽ ἄγαν
   πρὸς τοὺς κακῶς πράσσοντας, ἄνθρωπος γεγώς

INO. Don't be disturbed too much when you see unhappy people; you are human too.

Stob. 4.48.4

fr. 7 (407 Kannicht)

IN.   ἀμουσία τοι μηδ᾽ ἐπ᾽ οἰκτροῖσιν δάκρυ
   στάζειν· κακὸν δέ, χρημάτων ὄντων ἅλις,
   φειδοῖ πονηρᾷ μηδέν᾽ εὖ ποιεῖν βροτῶν

INO. It is really too rigid not to shed any tear for the pitiful miseries of others. Likewise, it is bad, while there is enough property, not to benefit any man because of miserable thriftiness.

1–3 Stob. 3.16.5 | 1–2 Stob. 4.48.20

First Stasimon

. . . .

Second Episode

fr. 8 (418 Kannicht)

ΘΕ(ΜΙΣΤΩ)
   γίγνωσκε τἀνθρώπεια μηδ᾽ ὑπερμέτρως
   ἄλγει· κακοῖς γὰρ οὐ σὺ πρόσκεισαι μόνη

TH(EMISTO). Be aware of mankind's condition and do not feel pain beyond measure. You are not the only human being who suffers distress.

Stob. 4.56.7 ‖ 1 γίγνωσκε τἀνθρώπεια Stob.: γίνωσκε τἀνθρώπια CPG 2.345.22 ‖ 2 κακοῖς Stob.: κακοῖσι CPG 2.345.22 | πρόσκεισαι Stob.: πρόσκειται *M*ᵃᶜ.

fr. 9 (408 Kannicht)

ΘΕ. ἐν ἐλπίσιν χρὴ τοὺς σοφοὺς ἔχειν βίον

THE. Wise people must live their life amid hopes.

Stob. 4.46.3

fr. 10 (409 Kannicht)

ΘΕ. μήτ' εὐτυχοῦσα πᾶσαν ἡνίαν χάλα
κακῶς τε πράσσουσ' ἐλπίδος κεδνῆς ἔχου

THE. Neither do you slacken all the reins when you are happy; and when you are unhappy, keep holding the hand of fine hope.

Stob. 4.46.5

fr. 11 (415 Kannicht)

IN. ἄνασσα, πολλοῖς ἔστιν ἀνθρώπων κακά,
τοῖς δ' ἄρτι λήγει, τοῖς δὲ κίνδυνος μολεῖν.
κύκλος γὰρ αὐτὸς καρπίμοις τε γῆς φυτοῖς
θνητῶν τε γενεᾷ· τῶν μὲν αὔξεται βίος,
τῶν δὲ φθίνει τε καὶ θερίζεται πάλιν

INO. My queen, many people suffer misfortunes; for some they have just expired, for others there is danger of their coming. For, the cycle is the same for earth's fertile plants as for generations of humans: the life of some people flourishes, of others it decreases and is harvested again.

1–5 Stob. 4.41.19 | 3–5 Plut. *Consololatio ad Apollonium* 6 (104b) ‖ 2 κίνδυνος: κίνδυνον *S*ᵃᶜ: 3 κύκλος γὰρ αὐτὸς Plut.: κύκλῳ γὰρ ἕρπει Stob. (= *Aeolus* fr. 22.3 Kannicht) | γῆς Plut.: γῆ *SMA* ‖ 4 θνητῶν τε γενεᾷ Stob. et Plut. codd. nonnulli: θνητῶν γενεᾷ/-ᾶς *X*² / *ΦΠΒ*: γενεᾶς θνητῶν *Θυ*: γένει βροτῶν τε *D* | γενεᾷ: γέννα Valckenaer | τῶν μὲν Stob.: τοῖς μὲν Plut. ‖ 5 καὶ θερίζεται Stob. κἀκθερίζεται Plut.

fr. 12 (416 Kannicht)

> IN. πολλοί γε θνητῶν τῷ θράσει τὰς συμφοράς
> ζητοῦσ’ ἀμαυροῦν κἀποκρύπτεσθαι κακά

INO. Because of their audacity, many mortals seek to keep their misfortune dark and conceal their troubles.

1–2 Stob. 3.4.9 ‖ 1 τῷ θράσει: τῷ πάθει A ‖ 2 κἀποκρύπτεσθαι: κἀπικρύπτεσθαι Trinc.

fr. 13 (412 Kannicht)

> ΘΕ. ἐμοὶ γὰρ εἴη πτωχός, εἰ δὲ βούλεται
> πτωχοῦ κακίων, ὅστις ὢν εὔνους ἐμοί
> φόβον παρελθὼν τἀπὸ καρδίας ἐρεῖ

THE. I wish for a friend, though a poor beggar and, if he so will, be worse than a beggarman, who, being all for me, will leave fear aside and speak what comes from his heart.

1–3 Stob. 3.13.12, Plut. *De Adulatore et Amico* 22 (63a) ‖ 1 γὰρ εἴη Plut.: γένοιτο Stob. ‖ 2 κακίων Plut.: κάκιον Stob. S, κακοῦ κακίων L.

fr. 14 (414 Kannicht)

> ΘΕ. φειδώμεθ’ ἀνδρῶν εὐγενῶν, φειδώμεθα,
> κακοὺς δ’ ἀποπτύωμεν, ὥσπερ ἄξιοι

THE. Let us spare noblemen, let us spare them; but let us spit on bad ones, as they are deserving of it.

Stob. 4.29.8 ‖ 2 ἀποπτύωμεν: ἀποπτύομεν *Mac* | ἄξιοι : ἄξιον *Mac*.

fr. 15 (422 Kannicht)

> IN. πολλοὶ παρῆσαν, ἀλλ’ ἄπιστα Θεσσαλῶν

INO. Many were present, but nobody can trust what the Thessalians say.

παρῆσαν Scholia Aristoph. *Plut.* 521b, Suda α 2154 Adler: γάρ εἰσιν Scholia Eur. *Phoen.* 1408 Schwartz | ἄπιστα Θεσσαλῶν Hemsterhuis: ἄπιστοι Θεσσαλοί Scholia Aristoph. *Plut.*, Suda: ἄπιστα Θεσσαλοῖς Scholia Eur. *Phoen.* 1408.

fr. 16 (410 Kannicht)

ΘΕ. τοιάνδε χρὴ γυναικὶ πρόσπολον ἐᾶν
      ἥτις τὸ μὲν δίκαιον οὐ σιγήσεται,
      τὰ δ' αἰσχρὰ μισεῖ καὶ κατ' ὀφθαλμοὺς ἐρεῖ

THE. A hostess is entitled to be given such a housemaid as will not remain silent about what is right, but who hates shameful things and will speak her mind before everyone's eyes.

1-3 Stob. 4.28.2 ‖ 1 πρόσπολον ἐᾶν Stob.: προσπολεῖν ἐᾶν Musgrave, Bergk: πρόσπολον νέμειν Dobree: προσπολεῖν ἀεί Collard ‖ 2 οὐ σιγήσεται Stob.: οὐ σιγῇ στέγει Schmidt 1864, 74 ‖ 3 ἐρεῖ Dobree: ἔχει Stob., Bergk: ψέγει Schmidt | κεῖ κατ' ὀφθαλμοὺς ἔχει Heath, Valckenaer.

fr. 17 (413 Kannicht)

IN.   ἐπίσταμαι δὲ πάνθ' ὅσ'εὐγενῆ χρεών,
      σιγᾶν θ' ὅπου δεῖ καὶ λέγειν ἵν' ἀσφαλές,
      ὁρᾶν θ' ἃ δεῖ με κοὐχ ὁρᾶν ἃ μὴ πρέπει,
4   γαστρὸς κρατεῖν τε· καὶ γὰρ ἐν κακοῖσιν ὢν
      ἐλευθέροισιν ἐμπεπαίδευμαι τρόποις

INO. I know well what a noble woman should know, to be silent wherever I have to, and to speak where it is safe, to see what I need and not to see what is unfitting, and how to rule my gluttony. I'm in troubles, but I grew up in freeborn ways.

1-5 Stob. 4.29.62 | 1-3 Orion *Floril.* 1-5 | 1-2 Plut. *De Garrulitate* 9 (506c) ‖ 1 ὅσ' εὐγενῆ Stob.: ὅσαις γενῇ Orion ‖ 2 ὅπου Stob.: ὅποι Plut. ‖ 3 πρέπει Orion: χρεών Stob. ‖ 4-5 om. Orion, *lemma* (ante 4-5) Kannicht, Collard ‖ 4 γαστρὸς κρατεῖν τε· Valckenaer 175: γαστρὸς κρατεῖν δέ· Kannicht | θράσους pro γαστρὸς Vitelli 476 | ὢν partic. masc, sing. ad feminam referendum vel de femina dictum dubium est: κἂν γὰρ ἐν κακοῖσιν ὦ Luzac, Valckenaer 175: καὶ γὰρ ἐν κακοῖς ὅμως Wecklein 43.

fr. 18 (411 Kannicht)

ΘΕ. ἴστω δὲ μηδεὶς ταῦθ' ἃ σιγᾶσθαι χρεών·
      μικροῦ γὰρ ἐκ λαμπτῆρος Ἰδαῖον λέπας

πρήσειεν ἄν τις, καὶ πρὸς ἄνδρ᾽ εἰπὼν ἕνα
4 πύθοιντ᾽ ἂν ἀστοὶ πάντες {ἃ κρύπτειν χρεών}

THE. And no one should learn these things which we need to be kept in silence. For, just as from a small torch one can fire the mountainsides of Ida, so, if you still say something to one person, all citizens can learn it {which, however, one ought to conceal}.

1–4 Stob. 3.41.1 ‖ 2–4 Plut. *De Garrulitate* 10 (507b) ‖ 2–3 (μικροῦ . . . πρήσειεν ἄν τις) Schol. Pind. *Pyth.* 3.66 ‖ 2 σμικροῦ Collard ‖ 3 πλήσειεν S^ac | καὶ πρὸς ἄνδρ᾽ εἰπὼν ἕνα Plut.: κἂν πρὸς ἕνα εἴποις ποτέ Stob.: κἂν (vel χἂν) πρὸς ἄνδρ᾽ εἴπῃς ἕνα Dobree ‖ 4 ἅ–χρεών (unmetrical) Stob.: om. Plut., del. Herwerden 1862, 52: οὓς κρύπτειν χρεών Dobree: ἃ στέγειν χρεών Enger.

Second Stasimon

. . . .

Third Episode

fr. 19 (403 Kannicht)

ΑΘ. (/ΑΓΓΕΛΟΣ)
τίς ἄρα μήτηρ ἢ πατὴρ κακὸν μέγα
βροτοῖς ἔφυσε κακὸν δυσώνυμον φθόνον;
ποῦ καί ποτ᾽ οἰκεῖ σώματος λαχὼν μέρος;
ἐν χερσὶν ἢ σπλάγχνοισιν ἢ παρ᾽ ὄμματα;
5 † ἔσθ᾽ ἡμῖν ὡς ἦν μόχθος ἰατροῖς μέγας
τομαῖς ἀφαιρεῖν ἢ ποτοῖς ἢ φαρμάκοις
πασῶν μεγίστην κακῶν ἐν ἀνθρώποις νόσων

ATH. (/MESSENGER) I wonder: what mother or father gave birth to the accursed envy, as a great evil for the human race? Wherever has it actually got a part in our body? May it have a residence in our hands or entrails or next to our eyes? †There is for us as there was† a great labour for doctors to remove by surgery or remedial potions or drugs this disease which is the greatest of all mankind's illnesses.

1–7 Stob. 3.38.8 | 3–4 Satyrus *Vit. Eur.* P. Oxy. 9.1176 fr.39 col.16.30 ‖ 3 ποῦ καί ποτ᾽ Stob.: ποῖόν ποτ᾽ West ‖ 6 φαρμάκοις Stob.: χρίσμασιν West 1983.

Third Stasimon

. . . .

fr. 20 (*Oxy. Pap.* 5131. 1-7)

XO(ΡΟΣ)] επτε.[   ]..τ.[
          ... χαυνα[

          ἄλλη συνε . [
          οἵδε γὰρ ἤκουσ[ι ...]. τ. [.] .ολ[
5   φοράδην τὴν βαρυδαίμονα[
          Κάδμου γενε[ὰν πρὸς δεσπόσ[υνον
          δ]ῶμα φέρ[οντες

CH. Other ... So, these ones! They have arrived carrying the miserable
descendants of Cadmus in their mother's palace.

5 <θέραπες> φοράδην Kovacs 2016 ‖ 6 post 7 transposes Kovacs 2016 ‖ 7a < –
ῡ υ – ῡ υ – –> post 7 add. Finglass.

Fourth Episode

fr. 21 (*Oxy. Pap.* 5131. 8-28)

ΑΘΑΜΑΣ
                θέσθ' ἡσύχ[ως νίν οἱ π[έλας πρὸ δ[ωμάτων
          β   μικρὸν μὲν ὑμῖν ἄχθος, ἀλγειν[ὸν δ' ἐμοί.
10   γυμνοῦτε, δείκνυτ' εἰς φάος πο[
                μὴ καὶ λεληθὼς ἐν πέπλοισιν[
                [_____]
ΙΝΩ
[τώ]δε ψυχα . . μοχ . [ ]   [
          α   [.]. . .[. . .]ακι . .[.]ων [
                .]. .[. . . . . . ἀ]εικέλιος ὦ ταλαπ[ειρι
15   κακ]ῶν δύστηνος [
                       ]ελι[[τ]] . .α . . α . . . . [
                       ]ανο[. .].   [
                                          ]ασ [

                                          ]ο δυστην[
20   stripped
                                          ] . ν . [

86

]. ροφαι[
].. αδεσ[
].. ωτλαστ[
25   ]ησασ[|εκ|].[
]   [
]ματω.[
].ονω.[

ATH. Gently bend them beside her, in front of the house. Their load is light for you, but painful for me. Uncover their bodies! Show them to light, for fear that I may be fooled about their death as they are covered with veils!

INO. My soul(s) ... How terrible and painful my life is! ... How unhappy I am through my miseries! ...

fr. 22 (404 Kannicht)

IN.   τό τ’ εὐγενές
πολλὴν δίδωσιν ἐλπίδ’ ὡς ἄρξουσι γῆς

INO. Their gentle origins give men much hope that they will rule over the earth.

Stob. 4.29.48.

fr. 23 (405 Kannicht)

IN.   τὴν εὐγένειαν, κἂν ἄμορφος ᾖ γάμος,
τιμῶσι πολλοὶ προσλαβεῖν τέκνων χάριν
τό τ’ ἀξίωμα μᾶλλον ἢ τὰ χρήματα

INO. Nobility, and even if a marriage is ill-assorted, many consider it honorable to obtain for the sake of the children, more for the dignity than the wealth.

Stob. 4.29.49.

fr. 24 (421 Kannicht)

IN.   κοίλοις ἐν ἄντροις ἄλυχνος, ὥστε θὴρ μόνος

INO. In hollow caves, without a lamp, like a lonely beast.

Pollux 7.178 ‖ θὴρ μόνος nos | θήρ, μόνος Kannicht.

Fourth Stasimon

. . . .

Exodus

fr. 25 (TrGF 2 fr. 100)

ΔΙ(ΟΝΥΣΟΣ)
πόντου πλάνητες Λευκοθέαν ἐπώνυμον

DI(ONYSUS) Travelers wandering the sea [will have protection by her as a goddess] named Leucothea.

fr. 26 (TrGF 2 fr. 101)

ΔΙ.   σεμνὸς Παλαίμων ναυτίλοις κεκλήσεται

DI. The sailors will call him by the divine name of Palaemon

fr. 27 (419 Kannicht)

ΔΙ.   βίᾳ νυν ἕλκετ᾽ ὦ κακοὶ τιμὰς βροτοί,
      καὶ κτᾶσθε πλοῦτον πάντοθεν θηρώμενοι,
      σύμμεικτα μὴ δίκαια καὶ δίκαι᾽ ὁμοῦ·
4   ἔπειτ᾽ ἀμᾶσθε τῶνδε δύστηνον θέρος

DI. It is through force that you attract privileges, evil people, and try to gain wealth by chasing it everywhere, from unfair and just works together; and then you harvest from them a crop of unhappiness.

1–4 Stob. (1) 3.10.23 et Stob. (2) 4.31.56 | 2–4 Theodor. Metoch. *Miscell.* 85 ‖ 1 βίᾳ νυν ἕλκετ᾽ Stob. (1): βίᾳ νυν ἐφέλκετ᾽ Stobaeus (2) ‖ 3 σύμμεικτα μὴ Nauck²: σύμμικτα μὴ Stob. (1) et Theodor.: σύμμικτ᾽ ἄμὴ Stob. (2), συμικτ᾽ ἀμ᾽ ἢ M, σύμμικτ᾽ ἃ μὴ A | καὶ δίκαι᾽ Stob. (1) et Theodor.: καὶ ἄδικα Stob. (2) ‖ 4 ἀμᾶσθε Stob. (2): ἀμᾶσθαι Stob. (1) S et Theodor. | τῶνδε Stob. (2) et Theodor.: τόνδε Stob. (1) S: τοῦδε A : τὸ supra δὲ scr. A².

fr. 28 (417 Kannicht)

ΔΙ.   κέκτησο δ᾽ ὀρθῶς ἂν ἔχῃς ἄνευ ψόγου
      † καὶ σμικρὰ σώζων τοὔνεχ᾽ ὃν σέβειν πρέπει †

μηδ' ὡς κακὸς ναύκληρος, εὖ πράξας ποτέ
ζητῶν τὰ πλείον', εἶτα πάντ' ἀπώλεσεν

DI. To get what you have without charge, †and if the acquisitions are small, keep them while respecting the one who deserves respect†; and do not follow the example of a bad captain who, after a good luck, is asking for more and more to lose everything.

1–4 Stob. (1) 4.31.102 | 1–2 Stob. (2) 3.9.2 ‖ 1 ἂν ἔχῃς A: ἀνέχῃς M, ἀνέχῃς Stob. (1) S (corr. Gesner): om. Stob. (2) S | κέκτησο … ἃ ἂν ἔχῃς dubium (Jebb *ad* Soph. *Ant.* 1278 ὡς ἔχων τε καὶ κεκτημένος): κέκτησο δ' ὀρθῶς· ἂν <δ'> ἔχῃς Dindorf (probantibus Wilamowitz [notae manu scriptae in marginibus exemplarium suorum ed. Nʲ] et Blaydes 1894): κέκτησό τ' ὀρθῶς ἄν <τ'> ἔχῃς Madvig 1.719 sq. ‖ 2 καὶ σμικρὰ σώζων τοὔνεχ' ὃν σέβειν πρέπει Stob. (1) S (κἂν σμικρὰ … τοὔνεκ' A, κασμικρα … τούνεχ' M): καὶ μικρὰ σώζου τῇ δίκη ξυνοῦσ' ἀεί Stob. (2) | τοὔνδικον σέβειν πρέπει Cobet 1858, 605 | κἂν σμικρὰ σώιζων, τοὔνδικον σέβουσ' ἀεί Nauck (probante Cobet 1860, 140): κἂν σμικρὰ σώιζων, ξὺν δίκῃ σέβων ἃ δεῖ Hense: κἂν σμικρὰ σώιζου τοὔνδικον σέβων ἀεί Cropp ‖ 4 πλείων' Sᵃᶜ, πλεῖον M | πάντ' ἀπώλεσεν: πάντ<α γ'> ἀπολέσῃς Valckenaer 177 Grotio duce : πάντα διολέσῃς Blaydes 1894.

fr. 29 (420 Kannicht)

ΔI.   ὁρᾷς τυράννους διὰ μακρῶν ηὐξημένους
        ὡς μικρὰ τὰ σφάλλοντα, καὶ μί' ἡμέρα
        τὰ μὲν καθεῖλεν ὑψόθεν, τὰ δ' ἦρ' ἄνω.
4   ὑπόπτερος δ' ὁ πλοῦτος· οἷς γὰρ ἦν ποτε,
        ἐξ ἐλπίδων πίπτοντας ὑποπτίους ὁρῶ

DI. You see that slight lapses bring down tyrants who have been strong for many years, and that one day is enough to precipitate some from their high standing and pick up others high. Wealth has wings; those who once had it are discouraged in their hopes and fall on their backs.

1–5 Stob. 4.41.1 | 1–2 et 4–5 *P. Cairo* 65445 | 1–3 Philostratus *Vita Apollonii* 7.5 | 2–3 Plut. *Consolatio ad Apollonium* 6 (104a) ‖ 1 ηὐξημένους Grotius: αὐξηθέντας Philostratus: ἠσκημ<μ>ένους Stob. S: ἠσκημένους M (signo interrogationis posito) et A / [.]Υ[…]ΕΙΝΟΥΣ *P. Cairo* 65445 ‖ 2 μικρὰ τὰ σφάλλοντα Stob., *P. Cairo*: ϲμικρὰ Valckenaer: μικρότατα σφάλλονται Plut. ‖ 3 om. *P. Cairo* | τὰ μὲν Plut.: τὸ μὲν Stob., Philo *De somniis* 1.154, Lydus *De mensibus* 4.7 | ὑψόθεν τὰ δ' ἦρ' ἄνω

Plut.: ὑψωθέντα δηρ’ ἄνω Stob. S, ὑψωθέν τα δ’ ἤρ άνω M, ὑψωθέντα δ’ ἦρ’ ἄνω A: ὑψόθεν τὸν δ’ ἦρ(εν) ἄνω Philo et Lydus ‖ 4–5 "ex alio loco petitos esse" suspicatus est Valckenaer 177 "nisi forte 5 fin. ὁρᾷς vel ὅρα scribendum," sed *P. Cairo* contextum satis confirmat ‖ 4 ὁ Stob. *S*[pc] et Trinc.: οὐ *S*[ac], *MA* | ποτε Stob. *ΣM* (om. *A*).

fr. 30 (423 Kannicht)

δ’ ἄρα;

And perhaps?

δ’ ἄρα; Kannicht : δ’ ἄρα· Hesychius δ 256.

———

Sigla

A	codex *A*
A[ac]	codex *A* ante correctionem
A[pc]	codex *A* post correctionem
A[1]	manus prima
A[2]	manus posterior
Trinc.	Trincavellus Stobaei editor (Venetiis 1535)
N[1]	Nauck[1]
N[2]	Nauck[2]

Bibliography

Alexiou, M. 2002. *The Ritual Lament in the Greek Tradition* (revised by D. Yatromanolakis and P. Roilos). 2nd ed. Lanham. Orig. pub. 1974. London.

Barrett, W. S. 1964. *Euripides: Hippolytos.* Oxford.

Bergk, T. 1833. *Commentatio de fragmentis Sophoclis.* Leipzig.

Bernabé, A. 1996. *Poetarum Epicorum Graecorum Testimonia et Fragmenta.* Stuttgart.

Bethe, E. 1900–1931. *Pollux: Onomastikon.* 2 vols. Leipzig.

Biehl, W. 1989. *Euripides: Troades.* Heidelberg.

Biggs, P. 1966. "The Disease Theme in Sophocles' *Ajax, Philoctetes,* and *Trachiniae.*" *Classical Philology* 61:223–235.

Blaydes, F. H. M. 1894. *Adversaria in Tragicorum Graecorum Fragmenta.* Halis Saxonum.

———. 1902. *Spicilegium tragicum: Observationes criticas in tragicos poetas Graecos continens.* Halle.

Bothe, F. H. 1844. *Euripidis Fabularum Fragmenta.* Berlin.

Brink, C. O. 1971. *Horace on Poetry: The 'Ars Poetica.'* Cambridge.

Bursian, C. 1866. "Zu Hyginus." *Neue Jahrbücher für Philology und Paedagogik* 93 (= *Jahrbücher für classische Philologie* 12):761–788.

Cameron, A. 2004. *Greek Mythography in the Roman World.* American Philological Association American Classical Studies 48. Oxford and New York.

Campbell, D. A. 1992. *Greek Lyric: Bacchylides, Corinna, and Others.* Vol. 4. Cambridge, MA.

Carpenter, T. H., and C. A. Faraone, eds. 1993. *Masks of Dionysus.* Ithaca.

Chantry, M. 1994. *Scholia Vetera in Aristophanis Plutum.* Groningen.

Chong-Gossard, J. 2016. "The Irony of Consolation in Euripides' Plays and Fragments." *Ramus* 45:18–44.

Clauss, J. J., and S. I. Johnson, eds. 1997. *Essays on Medea in Myth, Literature, Philosophy, and Art.* Princeton.

Cobet, C. G. 1858. *Novae Lectiones quibus continentur observations criticae in scriptores Graecos.* Leiden.

———. 1860. "Stobaei ad Florilegium." *Mnemosyne* 9:86–148.

Collard, C., M. J. Cropp, and K. H. Kee. 1995. *Euripides: Selected Fragmentary Plays.* Vol. 1. Warminster. Repr. 1997.

———. 2004. *Euripides: Selected Fragmentary Plays.* Vol. 2. Oxford.

Collard, C. and M. J. Cropp. 2008a. *Euripides: Fragments. Vol. 1, Aegeus-Meleager.* Cambridge, MA.

———. 2008b. *Euripides: Fragments. Vol. 2, Oedipus-Chrysippus, Other Fragments.* Cambridge, MA.

Conomis, N. C. 1970. *Lycurgi Oratione in Leocratem cum Ceterarum Lycurgi Orationum Fragmentis.* Leipzig.

Conzález, von M. C. 2017. *Der Mythos des Athamas in der griechischen und lateinischen Literatur.* Classica Monacensia 51. Tübingen.

Cropp, M. J. 2013. *Euripides: Electra. With Introduction, Translation and Commentary.* Warminster. Orig. Pub. 1988.

Cropp, M., and G. Fick. 1985. *Resolutions and Chronology in Euripides: The Fragmentary Tragedies.* Bulletin of the Institute of Classical Studies Suppl. 43. London.

Davies, M. 1991. *Sophocles: Trachiniae.* Oxford.

di Gregorio, L. 1980. "Lettura diretta e utilizzazione di fonti intermedie nelle citazioni Plutarchee dei tre grandi tragic." *Aevum* 54:46–79.

Diels, H. and W. Kranz. 1952–1996. *Die Fragmente der Vorsokratiker.* 3 vols. Zürich.

Dietze, J. 1894. "Zur Schriftstellerei des Mythographen Hyginus." *Rheinisches Museum für Philologie:*21–36.

Dindorf, W. 1830. *Poetarum Scenicorum Graecorum, Aeschyli, Sophoclis, Euripidis et Aristophanis, fabulae superstites et perditarum fragmenta.* Lipsiae.

Dobree, P. P. 1833. *Adversaria.* ed. J. Scholefield. Cambridge.

Drachmann, A. B. 1997. *Scholia Vetera in Pindari Carmina.* Leipzig. Orig. Pub. 1903.

Easterling, P. E. 1982. *Sophocles: Trachiniae.* Cambridge.

Edmonds, J. M. 1931. *Elegy and Iambus: With an English Translation.* Cambridge, MA.

Eisner, R. 1979. "Euripides' Use of Myth." *Arethusa* 12:153–174.

Elmsley, P. 1813. *Euripidis Heraclidae.* Leipzig.

Enger, R. 1863. *Adnotationes ad Tragicorum Graecorum Fragmenta.* Ostrowo.

Erfurt, K. G. A. 1844. *Ioannis Stobaei Anthologium: Libri duo posteriores.* Berolini.

Farmer, M. C. 2017. *Tragedy on the Comic Stage.* Oxford.

Farnell, L. R. 1916. "Ino-Leucothea." *Journal of Hellenic Studies* 36:36–44.

———. 1921. *Greek Hero Cults and Ideas of Immortality.* Oxford.

Fassino, M. 1999. "Revisione di P. Stras. W.G. 304–307: nuovi frammenti della Medea e di un' altra tragedia di Euripide." *Zeitschrift für Papyrologie Epigraphik* 127:1–46.

Finglass, P. J. 2007. *Pindar: Pythian Eleven.* Cambridge Classical Texts and Commentaries 45. Cambridge.

———. 2014. "A New Fragment of Euripides' Ino." *Zeitschrift für Papyrologie Epigraphik* 189:65–82.

————. 2016. "Mistaken Identity in Euripides' *Ino*." In *Wisdom and Folly in Euripides*, ed. P. Kyriakou and A. Rengakos, 299–318. Berlin and Boston.

Finkelberg, M. 2006. "Ino-Leukothea between East and West." *Journal of Ancient Near Eastern Religions* 6:105–121.

Fletcher, K. F. 2005. *Ovid, Mythography, and the Translation of Myth*. Michigan.

Fontenrose, J. 1948. "The Sorrows of Ino and of Procne." *Transactions and Proceedings of the American Philological Association* 79:125–167.

Fowler, R. L. 2013. *Early Greek Mythography. Vol. 2, Commentary*. Oxford.

Frazer, J. G. 1921. *Apollodorus: The Library*. 2 vols. Cambridge, MA.

Gantz, T. 1993. *Early Greek Myth: A Guide to Literary and Artistic Sources*. Baltimore.

Garland, R. 2001. *The Greek Way of Death*. 2nd ed. Ithaca. Orig. pub. 1985.

Gesner, C. 1543. *Florilegii Stobaei*. Zürich.

Graf, F. 1997. "Medea, the Enchantress from Afar: Remarks on a Well-Known Myth." In Clauss and Johnson 1997:21–43.

Grotius, H. 1623. *Dicta poetarum quae apud Stobaeum extant: Emendata et Latino carmine reddita*. Paris.

Guardasole, A. 2000. *Tragedia e Medicina nell' Atene del V Secolo A.C.* Naples.

Guéraud, O. and P. Jouguet. 1938. *Un livre d' écolier et du III siècle av. J.-C.* Cairo.

Harrison, A. R. W. 1968–1971. *The Law of Athens*. 2 vols. Oxford.

Hartung, J. A. 1843. *Euripides Restitutus sive Scriptorum Euripidis Ingeniique Censura*. 2 vols. Hamburg.

Headlam, W. 1893. "Various Conjectures." *Journal of Philology* 21:75–100.

Heath, B. 1762. *Notae sive lectiones ad tragicorum veterum … dramata*. Oxford.

Hense, O. 1868. *Exercitationes criticae imprimis in Euripidis fragmenta*. Halis.

Hense, O. and C. Wachsmuth. 1894–1912. *Ioannis Stobaei Anthologium: contain the 'Florilegium'*. 5 vols. Berlin.

Henrichs, A. 1978. "Greek Maenadism from Olympias to Messalina." *Harvard Studies in Classical Philology* 82:121–160.

Hercher, R. 1864. *Claudii Aeliani De natura animalium libri XVII*. Leipzig.

Herwerden, H. van. 1862. *Exercitationes criticae in poeticis et prossaicis quibusdam Atticorum monumentis*. 2 vols. The Hague.

————. 1873–1874. *Adnotationes criticae et exegeticae ad Euripidem*. 2 vols. Amsterdam.

Huys, M. 1996. "Euripides and the 'Tales from Euripides': Sources of the Fabulae of Ps-Hyginus? (Part 1)." *Archiv für Papyrusforschung und verwandte Gebiete* 42:168–178.

————. 1997. "Euripides and the 'Tales from Euripides': Sources of the Fabulae of Ps-Hyginus? (Part 2)." *Archiv für Papyrusforschung und verwandte Gebiete* 43:11–30.

Jebb, R. C. 1883–1890. *Sophocles: The Plays and Fragments. With … Commentary and Translation …* 7 vols. Cambridge.

Jocelyn, H. D. 1967. *The Tragedies of Ennius: The Fragments: Edited with an Introduction.* Cambridge.

Johnston, S. I. 1997. "Corinthian Medea and the Cult of Hera Akraia." In Clauss and Johnson 1997:44–70.

Jones, H. L. 1924. *The Geography of Strabo.* Cambridge, MA.

Jouan, F., and H. van Looy. 2002. *Euripide Tragédies. Vol. 3. 2, Fragments de Bellérophon à Protésilas.* Paris.

Kannicht, R. 2004. *Tragicorum Graecorum Fragmenta.* 2 vols. Göttingen.

Karamanou, I. 2006. *Euripides: Danae and Dictys.* Leipzig.

———. 2017. *Euripides, Alexandros: Introduction, Text and Commentary.* Berlin.

Keil, H. 1855–1880. *Charisius: Grammar.* Leipzig.

———. 1864. *Grammatici Latini.* Vol. 6. Leipzig.

Koonce, D. M. 1962. *Formal Lamentation for the Dead in Greek Tragedy.* PhD diss. University of Pennsylvania.

Kosak, J. C. 2004. *Heroic Measures: Hippocratic Medicine in the Making of Euripidean Tragedy.* Leiden.

Koster, W. J. W. 1969–1982. *Scholia in Aristophanen.* Groningen.

Kovacs, D. 1994. *Euripides: Cyclops, Alcestis, Medea.* Cambridge, MA.

———. 1995. *Euripides: Children of Heracles, Hippolytus, Andromache, Hecuba.* Cambridge, MA.

———. 2016. "Notes on a New Fragment of Euripides' *Ino* (P. Oxy. 5131)." *Zeitschrift für Papyrologie und Epigraphik* 199:3–6.

Kowalzig, B. 2013. "Dancing Dolphins." In *Dithyramb in Context*, ed. B. Kowalzig and P. Wilson, 31–58. Oxford.

Krause, J. 1976. Ἄλλοτε ἄλλος: *Untersuchungen zum Motiv des Schicksalswechsels in der griechische Dichtung bis zu Euripides.* Tuduv-Studien 4. Münich.

Lape, S. 2010. *Race and Citizen Identity in the Classical Athenian Democracy.* Cambridge.

Latte, K. 1953–1966. *Hesychii Alexandrini Lexicon.* Copenhagen.

Lee, M. M. 2012. "Dress and Adornment in Archaic and Classical Greece." In *A Companion to Women in the Ancient world*, ed. S. L. James and S. Dillon, 179–203. Malden.

Littlewood, R. J. 2006. *A Commentary on Ovid's Fasti, Book 6.* Oxford.

Lloyd, M. 1994. *Euripides: Andromache.* Warminster.

Luppe, W. 1984. "Euripides-Hypotheseis in den Hygin-Fabeln 'Antiope' und 'Ino'?" *Philologus* 128:41–59.

Luppe, W. and W. B. Henry. 2012. "5131. Tragedy (Euripides Ino?)." *The Oxyrhynchus Papyri* 78:19–25.

Lyons, D. 2014. *Gender and Immortality: Heroines in Ancient Greek Myth and Cult.* Princeton.

Macias, S. 2012. "Pharmaka: Medicine, Magic and Folk: Medicine in the Work of Euripides." In *Greek Science in the Long Run: Essays on the Greek Scientific Tradition (4th c. BCE–17th c. CE)*, ed. P. Olmos, 249–264. Cambridge.

Madvig, J. N. 1871–1884. *Adversaria Critica ad Scriptores Graecos et Latinos.* 3 vols. Hauniae.

Manuwald, G. 2015. "Editing Roman (Republican) Tragedy: Challenges and Possible Solutions." In *Brill's Companion to Roman Tragedy*, ed. G. W. M. Harrison, 3–23. Leiden.

Marshall, C. W. 2009. "Sophocles' *Chryshes* and the Date of *Iphigenia in Tauris*." In *The Play of Texts and Fragments: Essays in Honour of Martin Cropp*, ed. J. R. C. Cousland and J. R. Hume, 141–156. Leiden.

Marshall, P. K. 2002. *Hyginus: Fabulae.* 2nd ed. Münich. Orig. pub. 1993.

Mastronarde, D. J. 2002. *Euripides: Medea.* Cambridge.

Mattes, J. 1970. *Der Wahnsinn im griechischen Mythos und in der Dichtung bis zum Drama des fünften Jahrhunderts.* Heidelberg.

Matthiae, A. 1829. *Euripidis Tragoediae et Fragmenta. Vol. 9, Fragmenta.* Amsterdam.

McDowell, D. M. 1971. *Aristophanes: Wasps.* Oxford.

McHardy, F. 2005. "From Treacherous Wives to Murderous Mothers: Filicide in Tragic Fragments." In *Lost Dramas of Classical Athens: Greek Tragic Fragments*, ed. F. McHardy, J. Robinson, and D. Harvey, 129–150. Exeter.

McKeown, J. C. 2017. *A Cabinet of Ancient Medical Curiosities: Strange Tales and Surprising Facts.* Oxford.

McNally, S. 1984. "The Maenad in Early Greek Art." In *Women in the Ancient World*, ed. J. Peradotto and J. P. Sullivan, 101–143. Albany, N.Y. (The Arethusa Papers. *Arethusa* 11:107–135. Albany, N.Y.: 1978.).

Meineke, A. 1823. *Euphorionis Chalcidensis Vita et Scrptis.* Danzig.

———. 1843. "Marginalien." *Zeitschrift für die Alterthumswissenschaft* 1:185–190, 289–296.

Mekler, S. 1879. *Euripidea: Textkritische Studien.* Vienna.

Mikalson, J. D. 1991. *Honor Thy Gods: Popular Religion in Greek Tragedy.* Chapel Hill.

Mills, S. P. 1980. "The Sorrows of Medea." *Classical Philology* 75:289–296.

Most, G. 2006. *Hesiod: Theogony, Works and Days, Testimonia.* Cambridge, MA.

Murray, A. T. 1919. *Homer: The Odyssey with an English Translation.* 2 vols. Cambridge, MA.

Musgrave, S. 1778. Εὐριπίδου τὰ σωζόμενα. *Euripidis quae exstant omnia. Tragoedias superstites recensuit, fragmenta collegit …* 4 vols. Oxford.

Nauck, A. 1889. *Tragicorum Graecorum Fragmenta.* 2nd ed. Leipzig. Orig. pub. 1856.

Newton, R. M. 1985. "Ino in Euripides' *Medea.*" *American Journal of Philology* 106:496–502.

Nietzsche, F. 1873. *Die Geburt der Tragödie aus dem Geiste der Musik.* Goldmann Klassiker 7555. Münich.

Ogden, D. 1996. *Greek Bastardy in the Classical and the Hellenistic Periods.* Oxford.

Pache, C. O. 2004. *Baby and Child Heroes in Ancient Greece.* Chicago.

Pack, A. 1965. *The Greek and Latin Literary Texts from Greco-Roman Egypt.* 2nd edition. Ann Arbor. Orig. Pub. 1952.

Padel, R. 1995. *Whom gods destroy: Elements of Greek and Tragic Madness.* Princeton.

Page, D. L. 1938. *Euripides: Medea.* Oxford.

———. 1968. *Lyrica Graeca Selecta.* Oxford.

Papadopoulou, T. 2005. *Heracles and Euripidean Tragedy.* Cambridge.

Parker, H. C. 1999. "The Romanization of Ino (*Fasti* 6.475–550)." *Latomus* 58:336–347.

Pflugk, A. J. 1831. "Zu den Fragmenten des Euripides." *Allgemeine Schulzeitung* 2:13–30.

Race, W. H. 1997. *Pindar: Olympian Odes, Pythian Odes.* Cambridge, MA.

Ribbeck, O. 1875. *Die römische Tragödie im Zeitalter der Republik.* Leipzig.

Rose, H. J. 1930. *Modern Methods in Classical Mythology.* St. Andrews.

———. 1933. *Hyginus: Fabulae.* Leiden.

Rose, P. W. 1995. *Sons of the Gods, Children of Earth: Ideology and Literary Form in Ancient Greece.* Ithaca.

Ross, W. D. 1955. *Aristotelis Fragmenta Selecta.* Oxford.

Sanders, E. 2014. *Envy and Jealousy in Classical Athens: A Socio-Psychological Approach.* Oxford.

Schadewaldt, W. 1926. *Monolog und Selbstgespräch: Untersuchungen zur Formgeschichte der griechischen Tragödie.* Berlin.

Schleiser, R. 1993. "Mixtures of Masks: Maenads as Tragic Models." In Carpenter and Faraone 1993:89–114.

Schmidt, F. W. 1864. *Analecta Sophoclea et Euripidea.* Neustrelitz.

———. 1886–1887. *Kritische Studien zu den griechischen Dramatikern.* 3 vols. Berlin.

Schmidt, M. 1871. "Verbesserungsvorschläge zu schwierigen Stellen grie-schischer Schriftsteller." *Rheinisches Museum* 26:161–234.

———. 1872. *Hygini Fabulae.* Jena.

Schwartz, E. 1891. *Scholia in Euripidem.* Vol. 1. Berlin.

Schwyzer, E. 1939–1950. *Griechische Grammatik.* 2 vols. Münich.

Seaford, R. 1990. "The Imprisonment of Women in Greek Tragedy." *Journal of Hellenic Studies* 110:76–90.

———. 1993. "Dionysus as Destroyer of the Household: Homer, Tragedy, and the Polis." In Carpenter and Faraone 1993:115–146.

———. 1996. *Euripides, Bacchae: With an Introduction, Translation and Commentary.* Warminster.

Segal, C. 1997. "On the Fifth Stasimon of Euripides' *Medea.*" *American Journal of Philology* 118:167–184.

Slater, P. E. 1968. *The Glory of Hera: Greek Mythology and the Greek Family.* Boston.

Slater, W. J. and M. J. Cropp. 2009. "Leukippe as Tragedy." *Philologus* 153:63–85.

Slavitt, D. R. and S. P. Bovie. 1998. *Euripides 4: Ion, Children of Heracles, The Madness of Heracles, Iphigenia in Tauris, and Orestes.* Philadelphia.

Smith, R. S. and S. M. Trzaskoma. 2007. *Apollodorus' Library and Hyginus' Fabulae: Two Handbooks of Greek Mythology (Translated with Introductions).* Indianapolis.

Sommerstein, A. H. 1983. *The Comedies of Aristophanes. Vol. 4, Wasps.* Warminster.

Stevens, P. T. 1971. *Euripides: Andromache.* Oxford.

Suter, A. 2008. "Male Lament in Greek Tragedy." In *Lament: Studies in the Ancient Mediterranean and Beyond,* 156–180. Oxford.

Valckenaer, L. C. 1767. *Diatribe in Euripidis perditorum dramatum reliquias.* Leipzig.

Vitelli, G. 1880. "Apunti critici sull' *Electra* di Eur." *Rivista di Filologia e di Istruzione Classica* 8:401–516.

Waern, I. 1985. "Derweinende Held." *Eranos* 83:223–229.

Waterfield, R. 2003. *Euripides: Alcestis, Heracles, Children of Heracles, Cyclops.* Oxford.

Watson, P. A. 1993. "Stepmothers and Hippomanes: *Georgics* 3.282–283." *Latomus* 52:842–847.

Webster, T. B. L. 1967. *The Tragedies of Euripides.* London.

Wecklein, N. 1890. *Dramatisches und Kritisches zu den Fragmenten d. griech. Tragiker.* München.

Welcker, F. G. 1839–1841. *Die Griechisch Tragödien mit Rücksicht auf den epischen Cyclus.* 3 vols. Bonn.

Wendland, P. 1962. *Philo Judaeus De Somniis.* Berolini. Orig. pub. 1898.

West, M. L. 1966. *Hesiod: Theogony.* Oxford.

———. 1980. *Delectus ex Iambis et Elegis Graecis.* Oxford.

———. 1982. *Greek Metre.* Oxford.

———. 1983. "Tragica VI. 13 On frr. of Euripides." *Bulletin Institute of Classical Studies* 30:71–82.

Wilamowitz-Moellendorff, U. von. 1893. *Aristoteles und Athen.* Berlin.

———. 1895. *Euripides: Herakles.* 2 vols. Berlin.

———. 1924. *Hellenistische Dichtung in der Zeit des Kallimachos.* 2 vols. Berlin.

———. 1931–1932. *Der Glaube der Hellenen.* 2 vols. Berlin.

———. 1935–1972. *Kleine Schrften.* 6 vols. Berlin.

Zeitlin, F. I. 1985. "The Power of Aphrodite: Eros and the Boundaries of the Self in Euripides' *Hippolytus.*" In *Directions in Euripidean Criticism,* ed. P. Burian,

52–110. Durham. Reprinted 1996, in F. I. Zeitlin, *Playing the Other: Gender and Society in Classical Greek Literature*, 219–284. Chicago.

———. 2008. "Intimate Relations: Children, Childbearing, and Parentage on the Euripidean Stage." In *Performance, Iconography, Reception: Studies in Honour of Oliver Taplin*, ed. M. Revermann and P. Wilson, 318–332. Oxford.

Zielinski, T. 1929. "Flebilis Ino." *Eos* 32:121–141.

Index Locorum

Subject Index